curriculum
connections

21st Century Science

The Universe

Published by Brown Bear Books Limited

An imprint of:
The Brown Reference Group Ltd
68 Topstone Road
Redding
Connecticut 06896
USA
www.brownreference.com

© 2009 The Brown Reference Group Ltd

ISBN: 978-1-933834-76-4

Editorial Director: Lindsey Lowe
Managing Editor: Tim Harris
Project Director: Paul Humphrey
Editor: Andrew Solway
Designer: Barry Dwyer
Picture Researcher: Andrew Solway

Library of Congress Cataloging-in-Publication Data available upon request

Contents

Introduction	4–5
Scale of the Universe	6–8
History of the Big Bang	9–12
The Inflationary Universe	13–14
The Infant Universe	15–16
Beginnings of Structure	17–19
Formation of Galaxies	20–22
Kinds of Galaxies	23–24
Structure of Galaxies	25–26
The Milky Way	27–29
Clusters and Voids	30–31
Active Galaxies	32–33
Energy Machine	34–35
Interacting Galaxies	36–37
Stars and Galaxies	38–40
The Sun	41–43
Colors and Spectra	44–45
Giants and Dwarfs	46–48
Binary and Multiple Stars	49–51
Birth of a Star	52–54
On the Main Sequence	55–57
Post-main Sequence	58–59
Stellar Nucleosynthesis	60–61
Supernovae	62–63
Neutron Stars and Pulsars	64–66
Black Holes	67–68
Open, Flat, or Closed	69–70
The Accelerating Universe	71–72
Accretion of the Planets	73–75
Large and Small Planets	76–77
Planets and their Orbits	78–81
Earth and Moon	82–83
Inner Planets	84–86
Life on Mars?	87–89
Distant Companions	90–92
Moons of the Outer Planets	93–94
Bits and Pieces	95–97
Beyond the Fringe	98–99
Forming Cores	100–102
How Atmospheres Evolved	103–105
Glossary	106–107
Further Research	108–109
Index	110–112

Introduction

21st Century Science forms part of the Curriculum Connections project. Between them, the six volumes of this set cover all the key disciplines of the science curriculum: Chemistry, The Universe, Living Organisms, Genetics, The Earth, and Energy and Matter.

In-depth articles form the core of each volume, and focus on the scientific fundamentals. Each article relates to those preceding it, and the most basic are covered early in each volume. However, each article may be studied independently. So, for example, the Chemistry book begins with some relatively basic articles on atoms and molecules before progressing to more complex topics. However, the student who already has a reasonable background knowledge can turn straight to the article about carbon-hydrogen compounds to gain a more thorough understanding.

Within each article there are two key aids to learning that are to be found in color bars located in the margins of each page:

Curriculum Context sidebars indicate to the reader that a subject has particular relevance to certain key State and National Science and Technology Education Standards up to Grade 12.

Glossary sidebars define key words within the text.

A summary Glossary lists the key terms defined in the volume, and the Index lists people and major topics covered.

Fully captioned illustrations play a major role in the set, including photographs, artwork reconstructions, and explanatory diagrams.

About this Volume

The science of astronomy has developed at an astonishing speed in recent years. It is hard to believe that the first attempts to explain the beauty of the night sky took the form of stories about gods and goddesses, heroes, and mythical creatures. Many ancient cultures used the stars as a focus for their mythological and religious tales. The planets, moving regularly across this background pattern of fixed stars, gave rise to the early "science" of astrology, which sought to link the fate of humanity with the cyclical motions of the Universe. Assuming that Earth was at the center of the Universe, astrologers observed and recorded these cycles with great care, until discoveries were made that could not be explained within the Earth-centered system.

With the assistance of the first telescopes, astronomy was born as a true science. With ever-increasing precision, astronomers observed, plotted, and cataloged what they saw. As larger and better telescopes were developed, and other instruments— such as photometers to measure the intensity of light, spectrometers to break it down into its various wavelengths, and cameras to record the night sky precisely—were invented, the Universe could be studied in exceptional detail. Invisible radiation from the stars, as well as visible light, gave wholly new information, and computers were used to analyze results and provide startling pictures of stars and galaxies. Our knowledge of what the Universe contains grew hugely in the late 20th century and continues to do so, at an ever-increasing rate, in the early 21st century.

To make sense of all the new data, astronomers turned for assistance to the physicists, and theoretical physicists have now proposed a model of the forces that define the basic rules of the Universe.

Scale of the Universe

The Universe contains everything that exists, from the book in front of you to the faintest galaxies that our most powerful telescopes can detect. Through history, our ideas about the size of the Universe have grown. At first, humans saw it as little more than the Solar System. But as telescopes got more powerful, the Universe expanded to the size of our galaxy, the Milky Way. In the 20th century astronomers first realized there were other galaxies beyond our own, and clusters of galaxies beyond that.

Spectral lines

Dark lines in the spectrum (range) of light given out by a star. The lines are produced when certain wavelengths are absorbed by elements in the outer layers of the star.

Spacetime continuum

A mathematical model that combines space and time. Einstein did this in his general theory of relativity.

Curriculum Context

For most curricula students should know that the red shift from distant galaxies provides evidence that the Universe has been expanding for around 14 billion years.

An expanding Universe

It is not just our perception of the Universe that has grown over time. The Universe literally is expanding, as the American astronomer Edwin Hubble discovered in the 1920s. When studying the spectral lines characteristic of particular elements in the light emitted by distant galaxies, Hubble found that every line had moved toward the red, longer wavelength, end of the spectrum, implying that the light waves had been stretched. This suggested that the galaxies are all moving away from us. In fact, however, the galaxies do not move—the spacetime continuum itself is expanding. Space does not expand on the Earth, within the Solar System, or even within a galaxy, but between groups of galaxies space does expand. The galaxies are driven apart just as currants in a cake mixture are moved apart as the dough rises.

As the Universe expands, the light waves from these galaxies are stretched, shifting them toward the red end of the spectrum. The farthest ones shift the most. This phenomenon is called red shift.

The Big Bang theory

If the Universe is expanding, in the past it must have been smaller, and may once have been infinitely small. This logic led to the theory of the Big Bang, the initial

Parsecs

One way of measuring the distances between stars is in light-years. Another unit sometimes used is the parsec. This is defined as the distance at which 1AU subtends an angle of 1 second of arc. (This is a very small angle; there are 60 seconds in one minute of arc and 60 minutes in 1 degree.) One parsec equals 3.26 light-years. The definition of the parsec is related to the method of measuring stellar distances known as parallax. As the Earth orbits the Sun, the position of nearby stars appears to move relative to more distant stars. Trigonometry is then used to calculate the distance between the Earth and these distant stars.

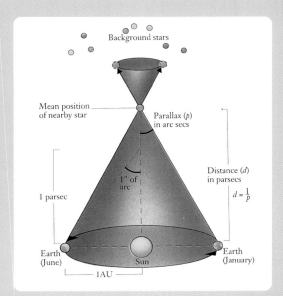

Background stars

Mean position of nearby star

Parallax (p) in arc secs

1 parsec

1" of arc

Distance (d) in parsecs

$d = \frac{1}{p}$

Earth (June)

Sun

Earth (January)

1AU

event in which the Universe and everything in it—space, time, matter, energy, even the laws of physics and the fundamental forces of nature—were created.

The scale of the Universe

To encompass the whole Universe we have to work with scales that appear very different from the ones with which we are most familiar—the scales of inches to miles, or millimeters to kilometers. The Universe looks very different on these different scales, but the laws of physics apply at all of them.

On a human scale we measure in tens, hundreds, or thousands of yards or meters. These may be conveniently expressed by exponents. The diameter of the Earth, for example, is 10^7m. The distance between the Earth and the Sun is about 93 million miles (149 million km), or one Astronomical Unit (AU). Mercury, the planet nearest to the Sun, has a mean distance from Earth of 0.39 AU; the farthest, the dwarf planet Pluto, is at a mean distance of 39.44 AU.

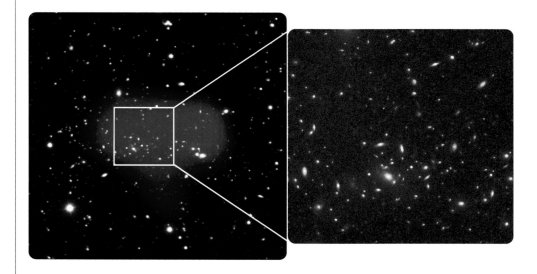

Two views of the distant galaxy cluster MS1054-0321. This massive cluster contains the equivalent of several thousand Milky Ways, and is 8 billion light-years from Earth. The image on the left shows the whole cluster. The blue region is an X-ray image, showing that this whole area is filled with hot gases. The image on the right shows a close-up of the center of the cluster.

Light-year

The distance traveled by light, moving at 186,000 miles/sec (300,000 km/sec), in 1 year. One light-year is a distance of about 59 trillion miles (95 trillion kilometers) or 63,240 AU.

When there are too many kilometers or astronomical units for the human mind to grasp, astronomers measure in light-years. Proxima Centauri, the nearest star to our Solar System, is 4.3 light-years away. A rocket traveling at 22,300 mph (36,000 km/hr) would take 100,000 years to reach this "nearby" star.

The Solar System exists in one of the spiral arms of the Milky Way—a galaxy 80,000 to 100,000 light-years in diameter, containing more than 100 billion stars, with the Sun at a distance of about 28,000 light-years from the center. The Milky Way is part of a cluster known as the Local Group, with a radius of about 2.5 million light-years. Its nearest neighbor in the Local Group is 160,000 light-years away.

The Andromeda Galaxy, at a distance of 2.3 million light-years, is the most distant object visible to the naked eye under good conditions. The Local Group belongs to the Virgo Supercluster, which has a radius of 50 million light-years.

History of the Big Bang

Astronomers believe that the Universe, including matter and space, was created in the Big Bang, and that the essential processes occurred in the first tiny fractions of a second after that event, when temperatures were vastly higher than in the Universe today.

People often ask what existed before the Big Bang and what the Universe expanded into. Yet the concept "before the Big Bang" has little meaning, because time did not exist until it was created in the Big Bang. And if space was also created, and if space itself is expanding, then it need not be expanding into anything.

Sequence of events

The Universe has been evolving ever since the moment of creation, and theoretical physicists and cosmologists have provided a description of the probable sequence of events that gave rise to the Universe as we know it.

In the very first instants, space and time were still forming. The forces of nature were combined into a

Curriculum Context

For most curricula, students should know that a 3K background radiation, or low-level microwave background "noise," exists throughout the Universe. This discovery has provided evidence for the Big Bang model of an expanding universe that is about 14 billion years old.

Forces and Particles

There are four basic forces in the Universe: the strong and weak nuclear forces, the electromagnetic force, and gravity. The strong nuclear force holds the particles together in the atomic nucleus. It is very powerful, but only over very short distances. The weak nuclear force is much weaker. It is associated with radioactive decay. The electromagnetic force is responsible for electric charge and magnetic polarity. It is the force that keeps electrons bound to atoms. Gravity is a weak force, but it can act over long distances.

Since the 1930s, physicists have discovered over 100 subatomic particles. However, all matter particles can be divided into two basic types, called quarks and leptons. There are six different kinds of quark, which can combine in various ways. The most important particles made from quarks are protons and neutrons.

Leptons are much lighter than quarks: they are almost without mass. Electrons are leptons with a negative electron charge. Another group of leptons that have no charge are called neutrinos.

single, primordial superforce. This period is known as the Planck time, and its details may never be explained, since the laws of physics were still being defined.

Inflation

By 10^{-35} seconds, space had expanded sufficiently for temperatures to have fallen to 10^{27} K, carried by extremely energetic photons. Gravity had already

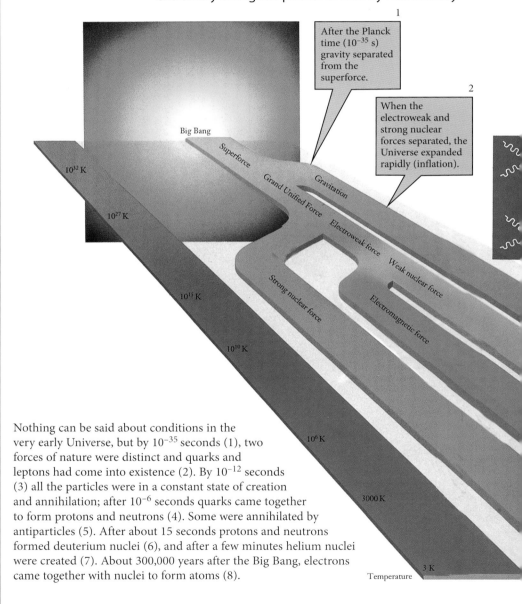

1

After the Planck time (10^{-35} s) gravity separated from the superforce.

2

When the electroweak and strong nuclear forces separated, the Universe expanded rapidly (inflation).

Big Bang

Superforce

Grand Unified Force

Gravitation

Electroweak force

Weak nuclear force

Strong nuclear force

Electromagnetic force

10^{32} K

10^{27} K

10^{15} K

10^{10} K

10^{6} K

3000 K

3 K

Temperature

Nothing can be said about conditions in the very early Universe, but by 10^{-35} seconds (1), two forces of nature were distinct and quarks and leptons had come into existence (2). By 10^{-12} seconds (3) all the particles were in a constant state of creation and annihilation; after 10^{-6} seconds quarks came together to form protons and neutrons (4). Some were annihilated by antiparticles (5). After about 15 seconds protons and neutrons formed deuterium nuclei (6), and after a few minutes helium nuclei were created (7). About 300,000 years after the Big Bang, electrons came together with nuclei to form atoms (8).

become a separate force, and the grand unified theory (GUT) force now separated into the strong nuclear and the electroweak forces, accompanied by the rapid creation of quarks, leptons, and their antimatter counterparts. This process caused the Universe to undergo a short but huge inflation (lasting 10^{-32} seconds) before resuming its previous rate of expansion.

By 10^{-6} seconds, quarks combined into pairs or triplets, forming mesons and baryons (including protons and neutrons): since that moment, quarks have been unable to exist independently. Their antiparticles did the same and then annihilated with the matter, but a tiny residue (one particle in every billion) was left,

Antimatter

Fundamental particles that have opposite properties to particles of ordinary matter, such as protons, neutrons, and electrons. If matter and antimatter particles meet, they destroy each other in a burst of energy.

3

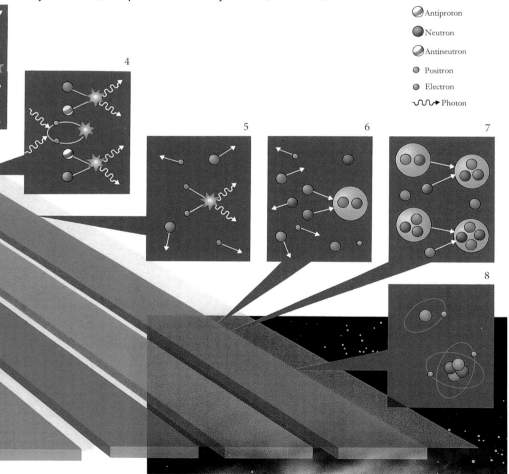

- Proton
- Antiproton
- Neutron
- Antineutron
- Positron
- Electron
- Photon

which went on to form all the matter in the present-day Universe. A large number of photons also resulted from this process.

Matter begins to form

At the end of the first second in time, the temperature had fallen to 10^{10} K; five seconds later neutrinos and antineutrinos had ceased to interact with the other forms of matter. After between one and five minutes, the strong nuclear force took hold, bringing neutrons and protons together in helium nuclei, preventing the neutrons from decaying into protons and electrons. The relative proportion of hydrogen to helium in the Universe was defined during this time. Energy levels were set so high that the atoms were entirely ionized and existed as atomic nuclei in a sea of electrons.

Matter and energy separate

Some 300,000 years after the Big Bang, temperatures had fallen sufficiently—to about 3000K—for electrons to be captured by atomic nuclei. As space was no longer filled with a sea of stray electrons, photons could for the first time travel large distances without interacting with matter: the Universe became transparent. At this stage, which is known as the decoupling of matter and energy, the cosmic background radiation was released. Atoms began to succumb to the force of gravity and collected into vast clouds, and the large-scale structure of the Universe began to evolve.

Between the release of the cosmic microwave background radiation and the present day, 14 billion years later, the Universe has expanded a thousand times, and matter has collected and condensed to form galaxies, stars (including our Sun), and planets. As this has happened, the Universe has continued to cool.

The Inflationary Universe

What we see today as the observable Universe began as a region of space no larger than an atom. The Big Bang, widely believed to be the event that created the Universe, occurred about 14 billion years ago. Astrophysicists have compiled an astonishingly detailed body of knowledge about what happened after the Big Bang, beginning only a tiny fraction of a second afterward, when the conventional laws of physics are thought to have been in place.

Combined forces

In the very early Universe the four forces of nature—gravity, electromagnetism, the strong nuclear force, and the weak nuclear force—were combined into a single superforce. Matter and energy were not the apparently separate entities they are today. Even space was constantly being broken and folded up because of the incredibly small volume that the Universe occupied. As time passed, the Universe expanded, and the single superforce separated into two components—gravity and the grand unified theory (GUT) force.

The next crucial step took place when the Universe was 10^{-35} seconds old. By this time, it had expanded and cooled sufficiently for the GUT force to separate into the strong nuclear force and the electroweak force (a combination of the weak nuclear and electromagnetic forces). Accompanying this separation was the sudden creation of quarks and leptons. This process was analogous to the way in which water vapor in the atmosphere condenses into clouds when the temperature of the surrounding air falls. The spontaneous creation of matter particles constituted a change in the Universe. It created enormous pressure, which drove the Universe to expand at a vastly accelerated rate. This process, known as inflation, bloated the Universe by a factor of 10^{26} (100 trillion trillion) in just 10^{-32} seconds.

Strong nuclear force

The force that holds the particles in the atomic nucleus together. Over very short distances, the strong nuclear force overcomes the electromagnetic repulsion between protons.

Weak nuclear force

A weak force in the nucleus that is associated with radioactive decay.

Visualizing the Big Bang

One of the most fundamental problems of understanding the Big Bang is that it is hard to visualize. This may be overcome by imagining the Universe as a flat piece of paper. The Universe is only two-dimensional, but we can make use of the third dimension to help explain what happened.

In the very early stages of the Big Bang, space was compressed so much that it had to curve through an extra dimension. In our two-dimensional model, this is the equivalent of screwing up the paper model of the Universe into a ball. This brought into contact regions that were far away from each other on the paper.

During inflation, space unfolded as the Universe expanded. In our paper model, the piece of paper is flattened out. Regions that were close when the Universe was crumpled up are now far from one another. The only deformation that now takes place in the flat sheet is the deformation caused by mass: this is the force we feel as gravity.

Timeline of the early history of the Universe after the Big Bang. The inflation of the Universe happened incredibly quickly, very early in its history. Since the inflationary period the Universe has continued to expand outward, but much more slowly.

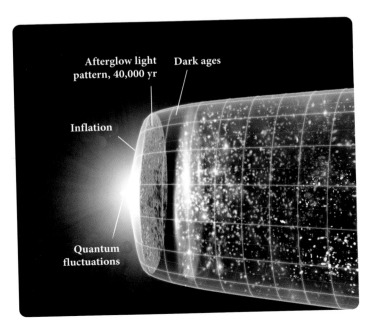

The Infant Universe

By the time the Universe was 10^{-12} seconds old, the electroweak force had separated to become the electromagnetic force and the weak nuclear force. Prior to this, all leptons—elementary particles such as electrons and neutrinos—had behaved in the same way.

Now, however, with these two forces (which govern lepton reactions) separate from each other, electrons and neutrinos became distinct from one another: electrons had an eletromagnetic charge, whereas neutrinos did not. Electromagnetic interactions began to occur between all charged particles, and photons began to be created in abundance.

Collisions and annihilations

The constituents of the Universe at this stage were in a state of constant collision and interaction. Particles of matter collided with their antiparticles and were instantly annihilated into a pair of high-energy photons. These photons soon decayed back into particle–antiparticle pairs and the collision–annihilation process started again. This back-and-forth conversion of matter and energy was possible because the Universe was so dense and hot: less than a millionth of a second after the Big Bang, the temperature was more than 10^{12} (10 million million) K. In this environment, quarks (the particles that make up protons and neutrons) could exist as separate particles, because any bonds they did make with other quarks were instantly broken by collisions.

When the Universe reached one microsecond in age, conditions changed. By now it had expanded and cooled sufficiently that the spontaneous creation of matter was no longer possible on the same vast scale it once had been. By this time, when the particles and antiparticles collided, the resulting photons did not turn back into matter.

Photon

A very small "packet" of light energy. At small scales, light can behave either like a particle or like a wave. A photon is a light "particle."

Antiparticle

All fundamental particles have a matching antiparticle that has opposite characteristics. For example, the antiparticle to the electron is the positively charged positron. If a particle collides with its antiparticle, the two are annihilated.

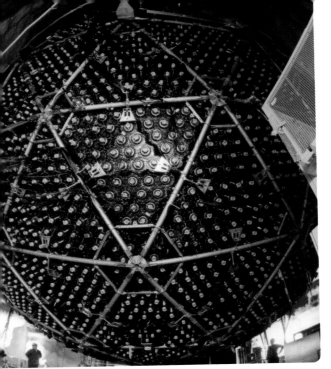

This giant sphere is buried 650 feet (200 meters) below ground in Sudbury, Ontario, Canada. The Sudbury Neutrino Detector is buried so deeply to screen it from the effects of other kinds of particles. It contains a special kind of heavy water, and detectors that are designed to pick up extremely rare collisions between the water and neutrinos.

Protons and neutrons

As the Universe cooled, the strong nuclear force pulled the quarks together to assemble as protons and neutrons. Most of these were annihilated in turn as they collided with their antimatter counterparts. However, there is a small but measurable tendency in the Universe to create more matter than antimatter. As a result of this, a residue of elementary particles remained. For every one billion particle– antiparticle pairs, one particle was created without an antimatter counterpart. This residue of matter particles makes up every atom or other particle found in the Universe today.

Neutrinos and antineutrinos had been in a constant state of collision with the other constituents of the Universe up to this point. As the Universe reached the age of 1 second, the neutrinos and antineutrinos all but ceased reacting with the other particles. This process, called neutrino decoupling, is potentially one of the earliest detectable events after the Big Bang. If we can build sufficiently powerful neutrino detectors, the decoupling could be detected as a background flux of neutrinos, allowing astronomers to study the Universe as it existed when it was just 1 second old.

Neutrinos

Subatomic particles with an extremely low mass and no electric charge, which move at close to the speed of light. Neutrinos can pass through matter without interacting with it, which makes them very difficult to detect.

Beginnings of Structure

As the Universe expanded, fractions of seconds after the Big Bang, its temperature continued to fall. When it was about fifteen seconds old, the temperature had fallen sufficiently to prevent electron–positron pairs forming spontaneously. In the same way that the neutrons and protons, and their antimatter counterparts, had annihilated one another to leave a small residue of matter, so the electrons and positrons now did the same.

Building blocks for atoms

Again, the small bias toward matter ensured that for every one billion electron-positron annihilations, one electron survived. This now meant that, for every particle of matter, several billion photons also existed.

Although the Universe was still dominated by photons and neutrinos, now it had also been seeded with the building blocks of atoms (protons, neutrons, and electrons). The Universe's entire quota of elementary particles was now in place, and they existed in a state of constant collision.

As the Universe reached an age of one minute, the conditions became right for neutrons and protons to begin to assemble into atomic nuclei (nucleosynthesis). This became possible because the collisions that now occurred, especially those between the baryons (neutrons and protons), were much less violent as a result of the Universe cooling and the particles no longer moving at such high speed, permitting the strong nuclear force to take effect on particles as they came into contact. Collisions between protons and neutrons built atomic nuclei through the process of nuclear fusion.

After approximately four minutes of nucleosynthesis, the Universe had expanded sufficiently, and the

In the late 1980s, and again in 2003, observations of the minute variations in this radiation using the COBE and WMAP satellites (WMAP image shown above), provided crucial evidence that the Universe was not uniform when matter and energy became decoupled. It consisted of hotter but thinner regions and cooler but denser regions of space.

temperature had dropped correspondingly, to stop the process. By now the "primordial elements" (those created in the infancy of the Universe, as opposed to those created later in the cores of stars) were made. These were atomic nuclei of hydrogen (a single proton) and its isotopes deuterium (one proton with one neutron) and tritium (one proton and two neutrons), plus helium (two protons and two neutrons) and its isotope helium-3 (two protons with a single neutron).

Neutron decay

Individual neutrons unattached to protons ceased to exist, because neutrons require the presence of other baryons if they are to remain stable. Outside the confines of an atomic nucleus, therefore, neutrons decay into a hydrogen nucleus (a single proton) and an electron. The difference in mass between the neutron and the combined masses of the electron and proton would have been converted into energy and carried away by a neutrino. The Universe was still too energetic for electrons to be able to bind to atomic nuclei. Any electrons that were captured by a nucleus were swiftly supplied with enough energy by collisions with photons to escape from them again. The Universe remained in this permanent state of ionization for several hundred thousand years.

Decoupling of matter and energy

At some age between 300,000 and 500,000 years, one of the most profound changes occurred in the Universe: the so-called decoupling of matter and energy. As the expansion of the Universe lowered its temperature, it became ever more difficult for photons to knock electrons away from nuclei. As the electrons were attracted to atomic nuclei, photons became able to travel large distances without colliding with other particles. In a sense, therefore, the Universe became transparent to the photons within it. The radiation released during this event is detectable today as cosmic microwave background radiation.

The decoupling of matter and energy less than half a million years ago is the earliest observable event in the Universe. The discovery of cosmic microwave background radiation in 1965 provided the first decisive evidence for Big Bang theory.

Gravity begins to act

Once the collisions between matter and radiation stopped, the force of gravity—so much weaker than the other forces—could pull the atoms together. This meant that the large-scale structure of the Universe began to evolve. Although astronomers have not yet fully resolved the details of this process, it is likely that clouds of atoms came together to form the various galaxies that dominate our view of the cosmos, and eventually areas within the clouds collapsed further to form stars with nuclear fusion at their cores. However, there is no direct evidence that this is true, because the oldest known quasars date from about 2 billion years after the Big Bang; astronomers have not yet been able to detect any objects older than these.

Curriculum Context

For many curricula, students should know that the cosmic background radiation provides evidence for the Big Bang model of the beginning of the Universe.

Nuclear fusion

A nuclear reaction (i.e. one between atomic nuclei) in which hydrogen nuclei fuse (join together) to form helium nuclei. There is some loss of mass, which is converted into a large release of energy.

Quasar

Quasi-stellar radio source. A very distant galaxy, not detectable in visible light, that is a strong source of radio waves.

Formation of Galaxies

The galaxies began to emerge, some 500,000 years after the Big Bang, from huge clouds of matter collapsing under the force of their own gravity. As they took shape, the material that they had accumulated began to collapse as well. As this fragmentation continued, the smaller lumps of matter formed stars. Thus galaxies formed at the same time as the stars they contained.

Curriculum Context

For most curricula, students should know that early in the history of the Universe, matter, primarily the light atoms hydrogen and helium, clumped together to form trillions of stars, grouped in gravitationally bound clusters known as galaxies.

What are galaxies?

Galaxies are huge assemblages of stars and other less luminous matter. Some galaxies contain nothing but old stars; others have regions in which new stars are continually created. Galaxies can contain many millions of stars and are found in many shapes.

The Sun belongs to the Milky Way galaxy, which has stars distributed in a flat spiral disk. With the exception of the Andromeda galaxy, every star visible with the unaided eye belongs to our galaxy. The misty band of light that stretches across the night sky is the combined light from the other, more distant stars in the disk of the Milky Way.

Only three galaxies are visible with the naked eye. Two, the Large and Small Magellanic Clouds, are satellite galaxies to our own. The third appears like a dim star but is a nearby spiral galaxy known as the Andromeda galaxy. Most galaxies astronomers observe through telescopes are at extreme distances; they look like misty swirls and patches of light and their individual stars cannot be made out.

Collapsing matter

After the decoupling of matter and energy, some 300,000 years after the Big Bang, gravity became the dominant force in the Universe and began to pull clouds of material together. This collapse is thought to have been a "scale-free" process during which large and small clouds of material were equally affected. The smallest regions finished collapsing first because they contained less material to be gathered together. In fact, the largest collections of matter, the superclusters, can still be observed collapsing today.

The period in the history of the Universe that came after decoupling is known as the Dark Ages. The reason for the name is that there were no stars in this era of the cosmos. As the nascent galaxies formed, however, stars naturally arose and begin to shine.

Galaxy types

Computer simulations of galaxy formation show that small, irregular chunks of galaxies formed first. These would either collide with one another or gently accumulate more material from their surroundings. When collisions happened, the stars in the galaxy building blocks were thrown into randomly oriented orbits, creating an elliptical galaxy. Those galaxies that continued to gently accumulate material, on the other

Two galaxies in the constellation of Hercules, caught in a slow-motion collision that will take millions of years to complete. Such collisions were far more common in the early Universe, when galaxies were smaller.

hand, developed into graceful spiral galaxies. At any time, however, if a spiral galaxy collides with another of comparable size, it will have its delicate spiral arms destroyed and turn into an elliptical galaxy.

Galactic centers

Observations with the Hubble Space Telescope show that most galaxies formed during the first few billion years of the Universe and, since that time, galaxies have changed little. There is also now a wide body of evidence that supermassive black holes exist in the centers of most, if not all, galaxies. A current focus for research is to discover when these formed. Supermassive black holes are not like the black holes made in supernova explosions. Instead of being extremely dense and only a few miles across, they are approximately the size of our Solar System and about the density of water. They can release violent amounts of energy, however, when they do swallow stars, creating intense activity at the center of their host galaxy and transforming it into an active galaxy.

Viewing the Dark Ages

At the moment, telescopes are not quite up to the task of looking back to the time of galaxy formation, but a number of new space telescopes are being designed and built in order to see into the Dark Ages. The Herschel mission is a 11.5-foot (3.5-meter) space telescope that is due to be launched in 2009, and the James Webb Space Telescope (JWST) is a 20-foot (6-meter) instrument due to be launched in 2013. Both will be more sensitive to infrared wavelengths, allowing them to see the first stars and galaxies. Another mission, called Xeus, is in development. This will be a 33-foot (10-meter) X-ray telescope, capable of seeing the birth of the supermassive black holes that sit in the hearts of many galaxies.

Kinds of Galaxies

Galaxies are found in a great variety of shapes and sizes, but they can be classified into two main types just by looking at them. Nearly all galaxies are either elliptical or spiral in appearance. Classification is normally made according to shape, following a scheme known as the "tuning fork" diagram, first devised by the American astronomer Edwin Hubble in the 1920s.

Elliptical galaxies

Elliptical galaxies are huge collections of stars that range in shape from perfect spheres to flattened ellipses resembling cigars. They include enormous elliptical systems at the centers of dense clusters of galaxies, containing up to one hundred billion stars. It seems likely that these galaxies grew so large by absorbing smaller ones that became caught in their vast gravitational fields. On the other hand, dwarf elliptical galaxies are some of the smallest star systems known, with only about a million stars. They are thought to be abundant, but are difficult to detect. Most of the stars contained in elliptical galaxies are old, and there is little interstellar gas or dust. As a result, very little star formation takes place within them.

Spiral galaxies

Spiral galaxies are beautiful objects, resembling pinwheels, which show definite signs of recent and continuing star formation. They contain a central bulge of older stars known as the nucleus, surrounded by a disk of material in which new stars are constantly forming. Where stars have formed in the disk, they shine with brilliant intensity and trace out spiral patterns around the nucleus. These spiral "arms" gradually rotate around the galaxy, following the compressed regions of disk material within which new stars are forming.

Curriculum Context

For many curricula, students should know that scientists catalog galaxies according to the coordinates of their positions in the sky, their shape, their brightness, and their other physical characteristics.

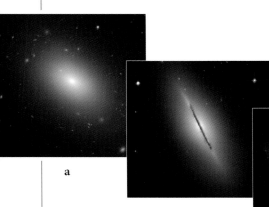

The four main types of galaxy: (a) elliptical; (b) lenticular; (c) spiral; and (d) barred spiral. The Hubble "tuning fork" diagram classifies these basic types further, depending on their shape. From Earth, similar galaxy types can look very different, because we are seeing them from different viewpoints.

a

b

c

d

Spiral galaxies come in a variety of types, which are normally classified according to how tightly wound the spiral arms are and how large the nucleus is. Approximately half of all spiral galaxies identified so far are barred spiral galaxies. These have a straight, barlike structure of stars that emanates from the galactic nucleus and stretches into the disk. The conventional spiral arms then twist around from the bar ends. The origin of the bars appears to relate to the gravitational interactions of the stars in a rotating spiral.

Other galaxies

Lenticular galaxies form an intermediate class of galaxy between ellipticals and spirals. They have nuclear bulges and a thin disk of stars, but they lack spiral arms. Galaxies with no obvious structure or nucleus are called irregular galaxies. Type I irregulars are galaxies which show evidence of spiral arms that have been disturbed in some way. A Type II irregular is just a confused jumble of stars. There is evidence that very small galaxies of this type, known as dwarf irregular galaxies, can be formed from the matter flung into intergalactic space during collisions between larger galaxies. Like spirals, irregulars are still undergoing the process of star formation.

Structure of Galaxies

The visible regions of a spiral galaxy were once thought to represent the system in its entirety. Astronomers now believe that the matter that has formed stars is no more than a tiny fraction of the total material contained within a galaxy. This other mass is contained in the form of faint objects, which are too dim to see from the distances we view galaxies, or other forms of matter that we cannot directly detect.

Among the matter that is too dim to see from Earth, the disk of a spiral galaxy contains vast lanes of dust and gas which are not illuminated. Sometimes dust lanes become visible because they block out the light from spiral arms and allow us to see them in silhouette form. The galactic disk also contains many fainter, older stars which cannot be seen because they are outshone by the young, bright stars in the spiral arms.

Halo of matter

From the visible evidence, it would appear that the bulk of the mass of a galaxy, like the mass of the Solar System, is concentrated in its core, or center. This would imply that, as the galaxy rotates, the stars that are farthest from the core would move more slowly than those that are closer to the center. Observation does not bear this out, however. Studying the way in which spiral arms rotate has led astronomers to believe that the bulk of the mass of a galaxy exists beyond its visible limits, contained in a huge, hidden spherical halo of matter.

Matter in the halo is thought to be contained in a number of different objects such as dim stars that have escaped the disk of the galaxy; failed stars, known as brown dwarfs; and the remains of stars that have collapsed and died, forming objects including neutron stars and black holes. Gas clouds are probably present

This composite image shows a large cluster of galaxies called the Bullet cluster. The main optical image shows the visible cluster of galaxies. The red area is an X-ray image, showing two clouds of hot gas that contain more mass than the galaxies themselves. And the blue areas are regions of dark matter, containing more mass than both the other regions put together. The area of the dark matter can be calculated because it distorts the light from galaxies farther away, causing an effect called gravitational lensing.

in the halo as well. The halo also contains luminous objects known as globular clusters. They are small, spherical collections of stars held together by gravity. They orbit the nucleus of their parent galaxies, and define a spherical region thought to indicate the limits of the galactic halo.

Globular clusters contain stars that are very old—most are thought to have formed about 10 billion years ago, but some are nearly as old as the Universe itself. Spiral galaxies typically have around 150 globular clusters, while elliptical galaxies can have up to 1000.

Dark matter

Beyond the galactic halo there exists an even larger spherical region known as the corona. This may be up to four times as large as the diameter of the galactic halo. It contains exotic particles, known as dark matter, which behave very differently from the five stable elementary particles. Although dark matter cannot be detected directly, its presence can be inferred by the effect of its gravitational field on the luminous matter in the galaxy. The corona could contain up to 90 percent of the total matter of the galaxy.

The Milky Way

Traditionally, when people talk of the Milky Way, they are describing the misty band of light that stretches across the night sky. The Italian astronomer Galileo (1564–1642) was the first person to look at the Milky Way with a telescope. He saw that it was composed of countless faint stars.

During the following three centuries astronomers came to realize that this faint band of light is our view of our own galaxy. The reason it looks so different from other galaxies we can see is that we are seeing it from within.

A spiral galaxy

The Milky Way is a spiral galaxy and is therefore relatively flat and disklike. If we look along the plane of the disk, we see many more stars than we do by looking to each side. The Sun, however, is not at the center of the Milky Way but is located in one of the spiral arms. The center of the galaxy lies in the direction of the constellation known as Sagittarius, and the spiral arms are named after the constellations through which they pass.

The Sun's position

Although the Milky Way formed about 14 billion years ago, the Sun was only formed in a spiral arm some 4.5 billion years ago, and has been in orbit around the center of the Milky Way ever since. It has completed roughly 21 orbits and is currently situated on the trailing edge of the Orion arm. As the name implies, this is the arm that contains most of the stars in the constellation of Orion. Some recent work on mapping the galaxy has suggested that Orion may not, in fact, be a complete spiral arm but simply an off-shoot that connects the Sagittarius arm and the Perseus arm. If this is the case, our location would be more correctly described as being within the Orion

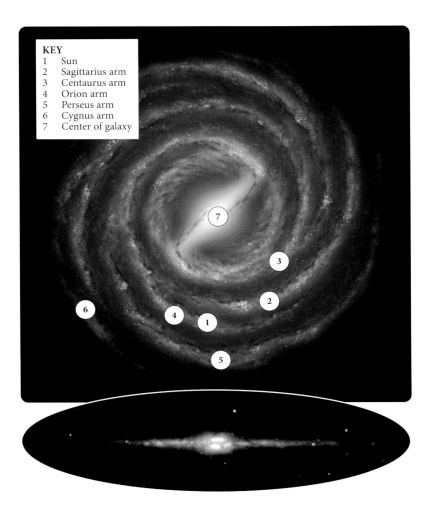

KEY
1 Sun
2 Sagittarius arm
3 Centaurus arm
4 Orion arm
5 Perseus arm
6 Cygnus arm
7 Center of galaxy

This illustration shows how scientists think the Milky Way would appear if we could see it from above. The center is shown as a barred spiral, according to the latest thinking. The image below it is an infrared composite of the edge-on view of the Milky Way we get from the viewpoint of Earth.

bridge or spur. The Sagittarius arm lies between us and the galactic center, while the Perseus arm curls round outside the Sun.

Galactic center

The galactic center itself is a place of considerable mystery, which is shrouded in dust and gas clouds. Visible light cannot penetrate these clouds, and astronomers rely on observations at other wavelengths of electromagnetic radiation, which can travel through the dust clouds. One of the brightest sources of radio emissions in the sky is an object known as Sagittarius A*, which lies at the galactic

A Barred Spiral?

Without doubt, the Milky Way is a spiral galaxy. Which type of spiral galaxy it is, however, remains contentious. For many years it was believed to be a standard spiral galaxy. But there may be a small bar joining the nucleus to the spiral arms, thus making the Milky Way a barred spiral galaxy. Another interesting feature of our galaxy's shape is that the disk of stars is not flat but warped.

center. The emissions almost certainly indicate the presence of a supermassive black hole. This has been calculated to have a mass of 3.7 million Suns concentrated into a sphere with a diameter smaller than the orbit of Mercury.

The Local Group

Like many large galaxies, the Milky Way has a number of smaller galaxies in orbit around it. The Magellanic Clouds are two irregular satellite galaxies, and there are a number of even smaller, dwarf galaxies caught in its gravitational influence. Beyond its overwhelming influence, the galaxy is gravitationally bound to others in an association of galaxies known as the Local Group. This contains 21 known members, spread over an area with a diameter of 10 million light-years.

Three galaxies in the Local Group are spirals (the Milky Way, Andromeda, and M33). The rest of the galaxies in the Local Group are ellipticals—including the giant elliptical Maffei I—and dwarfs. The gravitational center is between the Milky Way and Andromeda. These two galaxies are moving slowly toward each other, and are predicted to collide in approximately 5 billion years.

Clusters and Voids

Almost every galaxy is associated with other galaxies through the force of gravity. These associations are known as groups or clusters, depending upon how many galaxies are involved. Our own galaxy, the Milky Way, is a member of the Local Group, which contains about 20 galaxies of various sizes.

Curriculum Context

For most curricula, students should know that there are billions of galaxies in the universe, separated from each other by great distances and found in groups ranging from a few galaxies to large clusters with thousands of members. Superclusters are composed of agglomerations of many thousands of galaxy clusters.

Cluster shapes

Clusters are found in a variety of shapes and sizes. Some are spherical; others are irregular and sprawl across space. The different types contain different types of galaxy. By studying the types of galaxy contained, astronomers can understand how the shapes of galaxies evolve—especially the way spiral galaxies become elliptical galaxies.

In spherical clusters, most of the galaxies are elliptical. These clusters resemble globular clusters but on a vastly larger scale. Instead of being composed of individual stars, they are made of individual galaxies. These cluster around a central concentration of galaxies and follow well-defined elliptical orbits, which regularly take them into these dense regions. Once there, spiral galaxies collide with each other and become elliptical galaxies. In some cases the central object of a cluster is a giant elliptical galaxy. These are known as cluster-dominating, or cD, galaxies. They are thought to have been produced by successive mergers of several smaller galaxies. Irregular clusters contain mostly spiral galaxies and have no well-defined shape or center of gravity. Their constituent galaxies rarely come into contact with one another.

Superclusters

Clusters of galaxies can also be bound to other clusters by gravity. During the 1980s, astronomers mapped the positions and red shift (and therefore the distance

away) of thousands of galaxies, which suggested that these are not spread uniformly across space, but build up into chains called superclusters, which sweep across the Universe. The Local Group is thought to be part of the Virgo supercluster, which has a diameter of more than 100 million light-years. Superclusters seem to be concentrated around huge spherical voids. This may relate to the "lumpiness" in primordial matter detected by surveys of the cosmic background radiation. The largest supercluster is a thin sheet called the Great Wall, which seems to cover a region more than 250 million by 750 million light-years.

The pinkish color in this image of the supercluster Abell 901/902 is a map of the dark matter in this large cluster of galaxies. The image shows that the visible galaxies lie within clumps of dark matter.

Gravity in clusters often overcomes the expansion of the Universe. The galaxies then move according to their gravitational attraction to each other. But superclusters are so large, the space between them must be expanding, as shown by the Hubble flow. This cannot be simple expansive motion, because of the force of gravity. Instead of growing uniformly, the superclusters oscillate gently as they expand with the Universe.

Hubble flow

The general movement of galaxies and clusters of galaxies away from observers on Earth, resulting from the expansion of the Universe.

Active Galaxies

Although strange and energetic phenomena have been detected at the center of the Milky Way, they are in no way comparable to those observed in active galaxies. Ten percent of galaxies are termed active. The nucleus of an active galaxy is often so bright that it outshines the starlight from the rest of the galaxy. There are many types of active galaxy, each with its own peculiar properties.

Emission spectrum

The different wavelengths of light produced by a source of light. Emission spectra can be used as an analytical tool. Lines within the spectrum at particular wavelengths indicate the presence of particular gases.

Curriculum Context

For most curricula, students should know that scientists have analyzed the spectrum of light from stars to show that most stars are composed primarily of hydrogen, a smaller amount of helium, and much smaller amounts of other elements.

Seyferts and QSOs

The first type of active galaxy to be discovered was known as a Seyfert galaxy, after its discoverer, Carl Seyfert. Seyfert galaxies are spiral or barred-spiral galaxies that have very bright nuclei. When analyzed spectrographically, Seyferts show strong spectral emission lines produced by clouds of hot gas. Seyferts are strong sources of infrared radiation, although not all of them emit radio waves. Type I Seyferts have spectral emission lines that indicate they are being produced by clouds of hydrogen swirling at very high speeds around the center of the galaxy. Type II Seyferts, although displaying hydrogen lines, do not seem to have fast-moving gas clouds.

Quasi-stellar objects (QSOs) are thought to be very similar to Seyfert galaxies except that the activity in their nuclei is much greater. They appear as starlike points of light in the sky (hence the term quasi-stellar object), but are obviously not stars when studied spectroscopically. They exist at extreme distance, as indicated by the red shift of their spectral lines, and are among the most distant objects known in the Universe. Like Seyfert galaxies, they can be "radio loud" (in which case they are termed "quasars", which stands for quasi-stellar radio sources) or "radio quiet" (the traditional QSO). The luminosity of a quasar can be a thousand times the luminosity of a normal galaxy. The surrounding galactic structure of the quasar has yet to be observed because it is so much dimmer than the active nuclear region; this is why the various types of active galaxy are commonly called active galactic nuclei (AGNs).

Radio galaxies

Another form of active galaxy is the radio galaxy. As the name implies, such galaxies are strong emitters of radio waves. Instead of a point source, the emission comes from vast radio lobes, located on each side of the parent galaxy. A typical spiral galaxy has a diameter of approximately 100,000 light-years, but a radio source can span tens of millions of light-years from lobe to lobe.

The final type of active galaxy is known as a blazar. Known also as BL Lacertae objects, blazars are similar to quasars in most respects, except that they display no spectral lines.

The fact that most active galaxies are at extreme distances indicates that they are young objects in terms of the history of the Universe, because their light has taken millions of years to reach us. This, in turn, leads astronomers to believe that perhaps all galaxies go through this active phase.

A giant elliptical galaxy, reference number NGC 1316, is producing two huge lobes of radio emissions, shown here in orange. The lobes are each 600,000 light-years across.

Energy Machine

The various types of active galaxies—Seyferts, quasars, radio galaxies, and blazars—all seem very different from each other. However, many astronomers now believe that they are fundamentally the same type of object. The reason they look so different is because, from Earth, we view them at different angles.

Gravitational well

Active galaxies need some form of central "engine" to generate the enormous amounts of power they radiate. Although there are many processes that can generate vast amounts of energy, an object falling into a gravitational well is the most efficient. This has led most astronomers to believe that, in the heart of active galaxies, energy is released because matter is being sucked down into a supermassive black hole.

Black holes

Objects in space that are so dense that nothing can escape from them—not even light itself. A black hole has such a powerful gravitational field that any stars, gas clouds, dust, or other matter that stray too close are swallowed up.

The material falling into the black hole does not travel straight downward. The rotation of the galaxy causes the material to be strung out into a disk, known as an accretion disk, from which the material or object can complete its journey into the black hole. The matter in the accretion disk rotates very rapidly, causing it to heat up and emit X rays and other forms of electromagnetic radiation. Because the accretion disk is so thick, the radiation cannot readily escape through it. Instead, it is beamed along the axis of the accretion disk, forming two jets of material. These collide with atoms in the intergalactic medium and shock them into emitting radiation at radio wavelengths. It is these radio-emitting lobes that are detected in radio galaxies.

Surrounding torus

Surrounding the accretion disk is a doughnut shape of dust and gas known as a torus. The torus is heated by the short-wave emission coming from the accretion disk. The material in the torus then re-emits this radiation at longer wavelengths. Gas clouds, which swirl around the central engine, are also heated by emission from the accretion disk and emit radiation detectable as spectral lines.

The difference between a Seyfert galaxy and a quasar is merely the intensity of radiation produced in its nucleus. The difference between these and other types of active galaxy is to do with viewing angle. In an active galactic nucleus viewed along the accretion disk, the bright central engine is obscured by the surrounding torus. Only the radio lobes are visible, and we "see" a radio galaxy. If, however, the object is observed along the disk axis, it is possible to look straight down the jet. We see radiation of dazzling but variable brightness—the characteristic form of a blazar. At viewing angles between those of a blazar and a radio galaxy, emission from the central engine and possibly the jets is observed. Also, emission from the hot gas clouds is visible. This object is a quasar. This unified theory of active galaxies is not yet proven, but it does present a very attractive theory.

This image of the active galaxy Centaurus A combines a visual image with data from X-ray (blue) and submillimeter radio (orange) telescopes. The jets of material shooting out on either side of the accretion disk can be seen clearly.

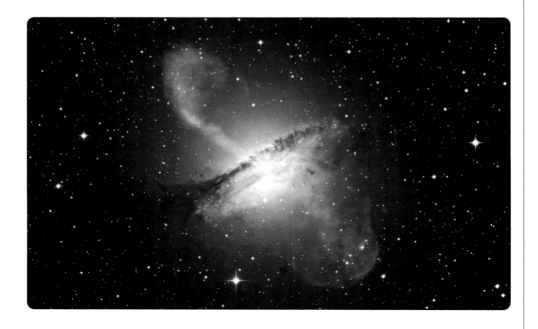

Interacting Galaxies

Galaxies in a cluster are constantly in motion (because of the mutual gravitational force between them and their neighbors), and so from time to time, perhaps once every several million years, they pass so close to each other that dramatic interactions can occur.

Similar galaxies

If the two galaxies are of similar masses, the results of the interaction are very different from those that occur when one galaxy is much larger than the other. If two spiral galaxies of similar mass fall toward each other, as they draw closer they begin to pull each other's stars from their orbits, and slowly the galaxies lose their spiral patterns. Some stars are pulled away from the galaxies and strung out in long "tails" through intergalactic space. Other stars are decelerated and begin to fall toward the center of mass of the two galaxies. If the galaxies pass sufficiently close, they merge and become one. When galaxies collide in this way, the stars they contain do not actually touch each other: the spaces between the stars are so large that the chances of collision, even in a galactic merger, are very slight indeed.

Unequal collision

If the two colliding galaxies are of very unequal size, then one is highly disturbed and the other remains intact. If a small, compact galaxy passes close to a large spiral, the spiral is relatively unaffected whereas the small compact galaxy is radically altered.

The effect of galactic interactions on the gas clouds contained in galaxies is rather different. Very often the new gravitational forces acting on the clouds trigger collapses that lead to an extremely vigorous burst of star formation—a phenomenon known as a starburst.

Some examples of the ways that galaxies collide over hundreds of millions of years. As the galaxies near one another, each begins to be distorted by the gravitational field of the other (1). As they spiral toward one another, streamers of stars are thrown out behind (2, 3). Eventually the galaxies may merge, forming an elliptical or an unusually shaped galaxy (4, 5). In some cases the two galaxies move apart again.

A good example is the galaxy named M82, which has been gravitationally disturbed by the large nearby spiral galaxy M81. Although the smaller galaxy has been significantly warped, it is undergoing a rapid bout of star formation near its center.

When galaxies merge, they are stripped of the dust and gas that make new stars. Merged systems are therefore not able to generate new stars. The motions of the stars are also disturbed, so that it becomes impossible for them to settle into the ordered regime needed for a disk galaxy. The random nature of the orbits tends to make the resulting galaxies elliptical.

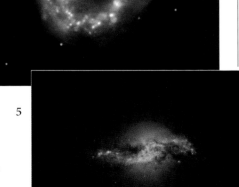

Stars and Galaxies

Stars contribute almost all the light that makes galaxies visible. A star is a large spherical concentration of gas containing so much material that nuclear fusion takes place at its core. The fusion of hydrogen into helium occurs because the weight of the overlying material provides sufficient pressure to force the hydrogen nuclei close enough for fusion to occur.

Nuclear fusion

A nuclear reaction (i.e. one between atomic nuclei) in which the nuclei of light atoms combine to form heavier ones. There is some loss of mass, which is converted into a large release of energy.

Curriculum Context

For most curricula, students should know that most stars are born from the gravitational compression and heating of hydrogen gas. A fusion reaction results when hydrogen nuclei combine to form helium nuclei.

Not all stars generate energy through fusion. For instance, if a potential star fails to gather enough matter to begin the reaction, it is called a brown dwarf star. A star may also be the hot remnants of a star that has finished its phase of nuclear energy generation. Examples of these are white dwarf and neutron stars.

Star variety

Stars exist in a very wide variety of sizes and luminosities. Looking up at the night sky shows how much stars vary in brightness. Some of the brightness variations seen in the night sky are due to differences in the distances of individual stars from us. The brightest stars in the sky have traditionally been recognized as patterns, which are known as a constellations. Although the brightest stars have traditional names, astronomers refer to them first by their constellation, then by assigning a Greek letter to each of its stars, starting with α (alpha) for the brightest star in the constellation.

Various types of stars tend to be associated with the various different regions found in spiral galaxies (such as the Milky Way galaxy, to which the Earth belongs). Spiral galaxies consist of a central bulge and a flat disk of stars. All the stars in a spiral galaxy's central bulge are old. They are called Population II stars and were formed when the galaxy was young. These stars are deficient in chemical elements heavier than helium (metals), which are only formed when massive stars explode. The orbits of the stars in the nuclear bulge have been flattened by the rotation of the galaxy. In color photographs, the nuclear region of a spiral galaxy is yellow, which is also a sign of stellar maturity.

Stars in the spiral arms

In the disk of the galaxy there exists a collection of both young and old stars. The most prominent features in the disk, however, are the spiral arms. These outshine the rest of the stars in the disk because they contain extremely young stars—some of which are less than a million years old and very luminous. These young stars are so hot that they shine with a brilliant blue intensity that is clearly visible on color photographs. They are known as population I stars. Unlike the older, metal-deficient Population II stars, they contain the metals that enhanced the interstellar medium when older stars exploded as supernovae. The Sun is a typical Population I star, since it contains elements heavier than helium.

High-mass and low-mass stars

The stars in the disk orbit the center of the galaxy. The massive blue stars that mark out the spiral arms are formed at their leading edges. This is where the interstellar medium is compressed sufficiently to collapse and form new stars. High-mass stars are short-lived, and after a few million years they explode as supernovae. Such stars do not complete a single revolution of the host galaxy.

A simulation of three rings of stars that have been recently discovered in the halo of the Milky Way. Two are the remains of globular clusters that have been pulled apart by the gravitational effects of the Milky Way. The third, larger ring is probably the scattered remains of a dwarf galaxy that collided with ours millions of years ago.

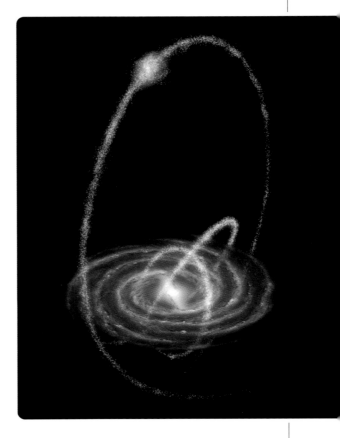

Dimmer, low-mass stars (like the Sun) shine steadily for billions of years and circle the galactic nucleus many times. As they do so they drift in and out of the spiral arms, unhindered by the processes that take place there. As the star formation process moves around the galaxy, the spiral arms rotate. This rotation is virtually independent of the individual orbits of the stars.

Halo stars

Stars are also present in the halo of a galaxy. There are old, metal-deficient Population II stars in the globular clusters, but there are also individual stars which wander this region of the host galaxy. Periodically, these stars cross the galactic disk and are known as high-velocity stars. This is because they have velocities that are high in directions at large angles to the plane of the disk, although they do not actually move faster than the other stars around them. The stars close to our Sun, which characteristically have such high perpendicular velocities, are only temporary visitors to the local solar neighborhood, and they will soon return to the halo of the Milky Way. There they will continue in their orbits until the force of gravity from the galactic nucleus once again pulls them through the disk and into the other hemisphere of the galactic halo.

Halo

The halo of a galaxy is a large spherical region that extends beyond the visible area of the galaxy. It contains some stars, and beyond these in the corona, hot gases.

The Sun

Without the star around which our Solar System is built, there would be no life. Our Sun has a diameter of 865,000 miles (1,392,000 km)—more than 109 times that of the Earth. It is a modest star, and shines with a yellow light that shows it to be stable. The temperature at the core is about 15 million K, forming an environment in which atomic nuclei are stripped bare of their electrons.

The photosphere

The outer layer of the Sun's atmosphere, called the photosphere, is the "surface" that is visible on Earth. Its temperature is about 6000 K. Viewed through suitable filters or by projecting an image of the solar disk onto a white board, the surface shows variations in brightness, referred to technically as granulation. The differences in brightness are due to the dynamic nature of the photosphere. Huge convective cells of gas rise and fall like boiling milk, and the surface undulates constantly. It is possible that hydrogen is undergoing a change from being completely ionized in the interior of the Sun to being neutral at the surface.

Some areas on the surface appear black, and are known as sunspots. These regions are up to 2000 K cooler than the surrounding surface. Sunspots are produced when magnetic field lines break through the photosphere and cool the surrounding gas. Sunspot activity on the Sun varies regularly over an 11-year cycle. There are also longer periods when sunspot activit is very low, or especially high. The variations in sunspot activity have effects on the climate on Earth.

The chromosphere

About 310 miles (500 kilometers) above the visible surface is the cool zone or "reversing layer." The temperature is at least 2000 K less than at the surface.

Layers of the Sun

The dense, hot core of the Sun extends some 109,000 miles (175,000 km) from the center. This is where the fusion reactions that power the Sun take place. The Sun loses 4 million tons (3.6 million tonnes) of mass each second through these fusion reactions. The core is rich in helium, which is formed during the fusion reaction.

Surrounding the core is a radiative layer rich in hydrogen, succeeded by a convective layer that transports material to the surface. The visible layer, or photosphere, is only some 250 miles (400 km) deep. Above this lies the chromosphere, and the highly rarified corona, which merges imperceptibly with space.

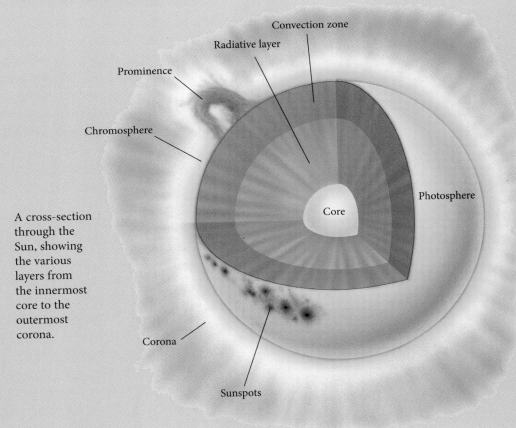

A cross-section through the Sun, showing the various layers from the innermost core to the outermost corona.

The gas here is transparent to most wavelengths of the radiation escaping from the photosphere, but it absorbs radiation at specific wavelengths characteristic of the atoms in that layer. It is here that the complex solar spectrum is produced. Analysis of this spectrum has enabled astronomers to determine the abundance of different elements in the Sun.

The cool zone lies at the bottom of a layer known as the chromosphere, several thousand miles deep, which envelops the photosphere. The chromosphere passes upward into the corona, which merges into interplanetary space and the solar wind. The chromosphere is visible optically only immediately before and after a total eclipse. It has a reddish color due to the emission of hydrogen. Studying this outer region with special instruments reveals that there are networks of jetlike spikes ascending from the chromosphere. Spectacular prominences rise up into the coronal regions, sometimes forming intricate arches and loops as they become involved with the Sun's magnetic lines of force. Gentle prominences may hang suspended in the corona for months or longer, while more short-lived, violent prominences may flare over 60,000 miles (100,000 km) into space.

Prominences

Huge streamers of hot gas that break free from the Sun's surface and flare out into the corona. They are also known as solar flares.

The corona

The corona is continually in motion, activated by shock waves sent up from the photosphere into the chromosphere. The corona's expansion into space gives rise to the "solar wind"—the mixture of rapidly-moving electrons, protons, helium nuclei, and other ions—which streams out through the Solar System and beyond. This may approach the Earth at velocities of around 310 miles/sec (500 km/sec), whereupon it interacts strongly with the magnetic field. The X-ray and ultraviolet radiation that reaches the Earth ionizes the upper atmosphere, producing the ionosphere.

Colors and Spectra

Even a casual observer of the night sky can often detect variations in the colors of the stars without a telescope. One of the easiest color differences to recognize is between blue stars and red stars. For instance, the two brightest stars in the constellation Orion are Betelgeuse and Rigel. Betelgeuse is a red star whereas Rigel is white-blue. In contrast to these two extremes, the Sun is yellow.

The color of a star corresponds to the temperature of its photosphere. Red stars are cool stars with a photosphere temperature of perhaps 3000 K, whereas blue stars are extremely hot, at temperatures of 20,000 K or more. White stars are also hot, at around 13,000 K. Yellow stars such as the Sun are intermediate, with surface temperatures of about 6000 K. For some stars, the wavelength at which most radiation is released is not a part of the visible spectrum at all. The peak emission of a 3000-K star is actually in the infrared region of the spectrum. A 10,000-K star has its peak emission in the ultraviolet.

Star Classification

Each star is given a letter to designate its spectral classification. In between each classification a number between 0 and 9 is assigned to graduate the steps further. The letters that astronomers use to classify stars are O, B, A, F, G, K, and M (agreed after the original sequence of A through P, proposed in the late 19th century, had been repeatedly revised and simplified). O stars are the hottest and most massive, with temperatures in excess of 35,000 K—they are blue stars. M stars are very cool, with temperatures of around 3000 K; these are red stars. Very cool stars are designated R, N and S. Another classification exists for very hot stars that periodically eject shells of gas from their outer layers. These are W, or Wolf–Rayet, stars.

In each of the spectral classifications there are stars of different sizes. Size also affects the brightness of a star. If two stars of different size have the same temperature, the larger star will be more luminous.

Temperature from spectra

Color is not the only characteristic determined by the temperature of a star. Temperature also determines which atomic transitions can take place within a star's atmosphere. These transitions occur when photons of light, emitted by the photosphere, are absorbed by electrons around atomic nuclei in the photosphere and lower chromosphere. These processes cause absorption lines to be superimposed upon the stellar spectrum.

Spectroscopy can be used to split the light into its constituent wavelengths, so that the absorption lines can be studied. Astronomers can then use the dominant absorption lines to determine which transitions are favored and hence calculate the temperature of the star.

Stars emit energy in accordance with Planck curves—graphs that describe the emission from hot objects, usually called black body radiation. The graph here shows Planck curves for stars with surface temperatures of 3000 K, 6000 K, and 12,000 K. The individual curves show the intensity of radiation emitted at different wavelengths. A star's color is determined by its temperature. Cool stars have their peak emission toward the red end of the visible spectrum, whereas hot stars peak toward the blue.

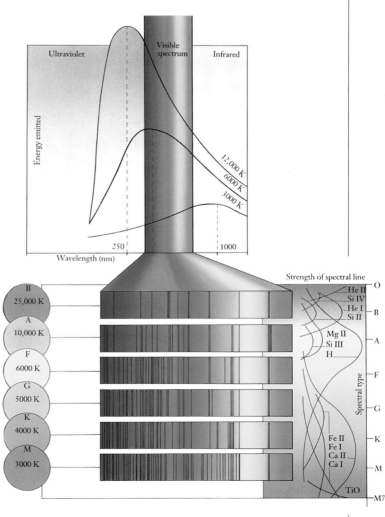

Giants and Dwarfs

Stars cannot be adequately classified by spectral classification alone. Although temperature is an obvious way to differentiate between stars, it does not give any indication of their size. Hydrogen-burning stars range from about one tenth the radius of the Sun to about 100 solar radii. As stars age, some grow to 1000 times the radius of the Sun. Stellar masses range from 0.08 times that of the Sun to 100 solar masses. It is unusual, however, for a star to have more than ten times the mass of the Sun.

Luminosities

Two stars of the same temperature but different sizes have different luminosities, which appear as subtle alterations in their spectral lines. To classify these differences, a system of five luminosity classes is used. Stars of group I are supergiants, II are bright giants, III are giants, IV are subgiants, and V are known as "main sequence" stars. The main sequence classification includes late spectral type (G, K, M) dwarf stars which are burning hydrogen, such as the Sun, which is classified G2 and is a yellow dwarf star. Any main sequence star with a K or M classification is a red dwarf star. White dwarfs are the remains of stars that have burnt through all their nuclear fuel: they are not included in this scheme.

Main sequence stars

The phrase "main sequence" derives from a pattern detected when astronomers devised a single chart on which to trace the characteristics of known stars. This is known as the Hertzsprung–Russell diagram. It plots the star's luminosity against its temperature.

The Sun resides on the Hertzsprung–Russell diagram at the point where one solar luminosity crosses the temperature of 5800 K, the temperature of the Sun's photosphere. If other stars are plotted in the diagram,

The Hertzsprung–Russell Diagram

Every star in the night sky can be plotted on the Hertzsprung–Russell diagram. Devised independently by Ejnar Hertzsprung and Henry Norris Russell during the 1920s, it is a graph of the brightness of a star against its spectral classification. Most stars—stable, "middle-aged" objects such as Sirius— are found in a curving S-shaped line from the top left to the bottom right. This collection is known as the main sequence. The largest stars are in the top right-hand corner of the diagram. The smallest stars are located at the bottom of the diagram. Red dwarfs are still part of the main sequence. White dwarfs are the dense cores of low-mass stars which have collapsed at the ends of their lives.

Stars vary tremendously in size, mass, and temperature. Stars at the same temperature emit the same amount of energy per unit surface area; brightness increases with size. Supergiant and giant stars such as Antares and Aldebaran are larger and brighter than the Sun—Aldebaran is about 25 times larger and 200 times brighter— but also much cooler (the surface of Antares is about 3000 K). Algol, a B-type star on the main sequence, is about 7 times larger than the Sun, but much hotter and brighter: about 11,000 K and 100 times brighter. White dwarfs such as Sirius B are about the same size as the Earth. They are fairly hot (about 10,000 K), but are 1000 times less luminous than the Sun.

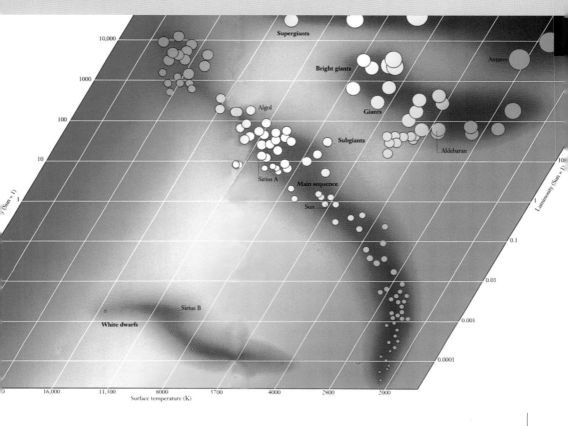

it soon becomes apparent that most lie in a curving S-shaped band that stretches from the low-luminosity red dwarf stars at the bottom right of the diagram up, through the Sun's position, to the high-luminosity blue stars at the top left. This is the main sequence, where stars spend the majority of their careers. The main sequence corresponds to the stable, hydrogen-burning "middle" age of a star's life cycle.

Aging stars

As a star ages, it begins to move off the main sequence. This is because its luminosity is caused by the energy released in its core by the nuclear fusion of hydrogen into helium. When hydrogen burning stops and helium burning begins, changes take place in the amount of energy released by the star. This internal change causes the exterior condition of the star to change as well, and it begins to change its luminosity and its temperature. Its luminosity goes up, because the star expands, but its temperature goes down, and so it moves into the top right-hand quarter of the Hertzsprung–Russell diagram. This is the domain of the red giant stars. It is here that old stars reside in the final stages of their history.

Following the end of all nuclear reactions, most stars end up on the bottom left quarter of the diagram where white dwarfs, the stellar remnants, are plotted.

Binary and Multiple Stars

Many stars do not exist in isolation; they have stellar companions and orbit each other. Occasionally it is possible to see the two components, either with the naked eye or through a telescope. In such a case the star is called a visual binary.

Not all stars that look close together are true binary stars. Some stars are not associated with each other and are located at vastly different distances, but because they lie in the same direction from the Earth, they look close together in the sky. True binaries are ones in which two stars are bound together by the force of gravity.

Binary systems

The time taken for binary stars to orbit each other is highly variable. It depends upon many factors, such as the mass of the two components, the ratio of their individual masses, how far apart they are, and what stage in their evolution they have reached. Some stars spin around one another in a few days, whereas others take centuries. Many double stars cannot be seen as visual binaries. Perhaps the star system is too far away for the separate components to be resolved, or perhaps it is relatively near but the two components are too close together. Sometimes one component is much fainter than the other and is outshone as a result.

The components of a binary star system orbit each other around their common center of mass—neither star is stationary. If this oscillating motion can be detected in relation to the background of stars, it indicates that a small or dim companion star is in orbit around a larger, brighter one. Such pairs are known as astrometric binaries. The best known of such pairings is Sirius A, the brightest star in the sky. A "wobble" in Sirius's movement indicated the presence of a much smaller white dwarf star called Sirius B.

Astrometric binary

A bright star with a much dimmer companion, whose presence is detected through a "wobble" in the orbit of the brighter star.

For much of their lives, binary stars simply orbit around their common center of mass (1). In the second stage of a binary star's lifetime (2), the more massive of the two stars has become a red giant. Material is ejected from this star by a stellar wind. The material crosses into the gravitational field of the smaller star, is captured, and spirals down on to its surface. This process increases the smaller star's mass. In the third stage (3), the red giant star becomes either a white dwarf or a neutron star. The once-smaller companion star is still on the main sequence, but it is burning its fuel much faster because of the extra mass captured from the other star. Finally (4), the companion star becomes a red giant, swells up to many times its normal size, and begins transferring mass back to the first star. If the transferred material falls onto a white dwarf, a nova will occur; if it falls onto a neutron star, an X-ray burst will occur.

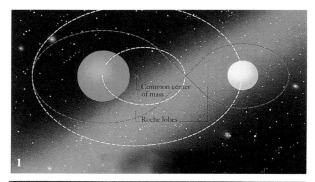

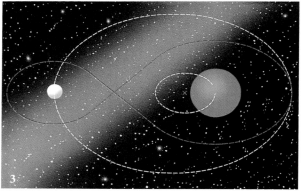

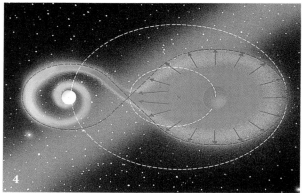

Spectroscopic binaries

Another method of finding binaries is to study their spectra. The spectral absorption lines may indicate the presence of two stars, each with a different spectral classification.

Even if the stars are exactly the same type, they are in motion, and this causes the spectral lines to alter in wavelength. This is because the wavelength of radiation emitted from a moving object is either stretched or squashed, depending upon whether the object is approaching or receding—this phenomenon is known as the Doppler effect. The stars are moving in different directions, causing the spectral lines to alter their wavelengths by different amounts. As a result, in the course of a single orbit the spectral lines move apart and come back together twice. If the companion star is too faint, its spectrum is swamped by that of the brighter star. That spectrum still exhibits the Doppler shift, however, and the presence of a companion can be inferred. This type of system is known as a spectroscopic binary.

Multiple systems

Triple star systems are also known, as are quadruple stars and systems with even more components. The more stars contained in a multiple system, the rarer they are. More than half of all the known stars exist in binary systems or in systems with as many as six members.

Spectroscopic binary

A binary star system detected by fluctuations of the spectral lines in the emission spectrum of a star.

Weighing Stars

Binary star systems provide an opportunity for astronomers to weigh stars. To do this, the distance between the stars and the time it takes for them to complete an orbit must be measured. Using simple mathematics, a figure for the combined mass of the two stars can then be calculated. An estimate as to which star contains most mass must then be made. If the two stars are identical, however, the figure can simply be halved.

Birth of a Star

Astronomers have studied so many stars that they have been able to build up a detailed picture of how they believe these fascinating objects "live" and "die". Stars change considerably over time—but this time is often measurable only in millions of years. For this reason, astronomers never actually see a star move from one phase of its life to another, much less witness a complete lifespan.

However, there are so many stars in the sky that it is possible to observe each of the individual stages by looking at different stars. From the observations astronomers make, they must try to deduce the correct sequence of events in a star's evolution and identify where each star is placed along the sequence.

Gas and dust clouds

Stars form within vast clouds of dust and gas. As these clouds orbit the center of a galaxy, they are tugged by gravitational and magnetic fields. How fast their constituent particles move depends on the cloud's temperature: the colder it is, the slower the particles move. Fast-moving particles resist collapsing together, and so stars can form only in the dense cores of cold clouds. Typically, these clouds are only about 15 degrees above absolute zero. Periodically, the clouds begin to collapse.

Chemistry in the Clouds

Complex chemical reactions take place within the giant molecular clouds in which stars form. Although the vast majority involve molecular hydrogen, the small amounts of heavier elements present also take part in the reactions and form more complex molecules. A particularly fascinating discovery is that giant molecular clouds contain organic (carbon-containing) compounds, necessary to the development of life. Astronomers are currently searching for amino acids and sugar molecules. If they prove to be abundant, it may give a clue as to how life arises in the Universe.

The trigger mechanisms for such collapses are thought to be collisions between giant molecular clouds or entry into galactic spiral arms. Both of these occurrences set up compression waves within the cloud, which cause isolated regions to become so dense that gravity overwhelms all other processes and the cloud collapses. These isolated regions can often contain enough mass to create several hundred stars of similar mass to the Sun. They are known as Barnard objects, and often appear as black regions in front of stars. Sometimes regions with emission nebulas reach the appropriate density and collapse. These appear as round, black "bubbles" within the glowing gas. They are referred to as Bok globules. As Barnard objects and Bok globules collapse, isolated regions within them collapse as well. In this way, the cloud fragments on many different scales. It is the smaller-scale collapses from which stars form.

Emission nebula

A glowing cloud of hot interstellar gas. The gas is ionized (charged), and emits light of various colors (most often red, due to the presence of hydrogen).

Protostars

At the center of the collapsing regions, concentrations of matter build up. Three-quarters of this matter is in the form of hydrogen gas. The rest is nearly all helium with 2 percent being made up of the heavier elements. This region is known as a protostar and, as material pours down upon it, the gas becomes so compressed that the temperature begins to rise dramatically. The rise in temperature makes the gas move faster and thus creates more pressure. This pressure gradually balances the inward pull of gravity and halts the collapse of the protostar. As more material accumulates on the protostar, instead of collapsing, it is squeezed gently. This raises the temperature still further.

Although there are no nuclear processes going on within the protostar, it is still giving off energy from the material that is striking its surface. This is given off as radiation but is very quickly absorbed by the dusty envelope raining down upon the surface of the protostar. This action heats the dust, which then re-radiates the energy at infrared wavelengths. The envelope that surrounds a protostar is vast; typically, it is 20 times larger than our entire Solar System.

The first young, infrared star to be found was discovered in the Orion star-forming region. It was discovered in 1967 by Eric Becklin and Gerry Neugebauer of the Californian Institute of Technology, and is now known as the Becklin–Neugebauer object. The youngest protostar, however, is known as VLA 1623, named for the Very Large Array telescope from which it was discovered. It is thought to be less than 10,000 years old.

The Elephant's Trunk nebula is a dark globule within the emission nebula IC 1396 in the constellation of Cepheus. This image from the Spitzer Space Telescope uses infrared detectors to show the glowing protostars within the obscuring clouds of gas and dust.

On the Main Sequence

As protostars accumulate more and more mass, the temperature and pressure in their centers grow ever higher until nuclear fusion begins to take place. This starts the processes by which the star generates energy, and the protostar begins to join the main sequence on the Hertzsprung–Russell diagram.

Balancing gravity and fusion

Before it can settle into stable "middle age", the star must adjust to the nuclear processes now taking place within its core. These processes provide a pressure that pushes material outward. Gravity, which has governed the formation of the star so far, is eventually equalized by the pressure of the hot gas inside the star, and the star stops collapsing.

Variable output

While pressure equalization is taking place, the star undergoes a dramatic and unpredictable variability in its luminosity and outflow of material. This behavior can also excite small regions of the surrounding molecular cloud, causing them to emit radiation. These emission regions, with a characteristic knotty appearance, are known as Herbig–Haro objects.

Star mass

The masses of the stars formed within the collapsing fragments depend upon factors such as the mass of material contained in the fragments and the rate at which the material accretes onto the protostars. In any collapsing cloud, the stars formed may range in size from the largest to the smallest known stellar masses.

In general, less massive stars are produced in much greater numbers than high-mass stars. Along the spectral classification sequence OBAFGKM, the most abundant stars are the red dwarfs with spectral types

Curriculum Context

For many curricula, students should know the evidence indicating that the color, brightness, and evolution of a star are determined by a balance between gravitational collapse and nuclear fusion.

The giant galactic nebula NGC 3603 is a cloud of dust and gas in the Carina arm of the Milky Way. Near the center is a starburst cluster dominated by huge, young Wolf-Rayet stars (stars that lose mass rapidly) and early O-type stars. Small, dark Bok globules at the upper left are probably in an earlier stage of star formation.

K and M. The high-mass, high-luminosity, short-lived stars of O and B type are very few in number, but these are highly important to the evolution of the star-forming region. These stars are prodigious in their release of radiation and generate intense stellar winds containing subatomic particles, which are accelerated along magnetic field lines away from the star. The radiation ionizes hydrogen in the surrounding envelope, creating free electrons and protons. When these particles reform into hydrogen atoms, they give off electromagnetic radiation. One of the common wavelengths for emission is in the red region of the optical spectrum and so these emission nebulas, often called HII regions, glow with a characteristic red color.

As well as ionizing their surroundings, high-mass O and B stars also push the surrounding material away from them. This causes the molecular cloud in their vicinity

to be compressed, and therefore starts the process of collapse in new regions. In this way, the process of star formation propagates throughout a giant molecular cloud, with regions of newer star formation associated with older regions. These are known as OB Associations.

Star lifetimes

The mass of a star determines just how long it spends on the main sequence. The more massive stars use their fuel at such vast rates that they only have enough hydrogen to last a few tens of millions of years. The lower-mass stars, despite having less hydrogen to fuse, exist on the main sequence for much longer because they use that hydrogen at a much more leisurely pace. A G-type star, such as the Sun, fuses hydrogen into helium for about nine billion years. A red dwarf star, which uses hydrogen very slowly, will continue to exist on the main sequence for tens of billions of years.

Star clusters

When stars emerge from their birth clouds, they are usually in associations known as star clusters. A good example of this is the young star cluster known as the Pleiades (Seven Sisters). After millions of years, stars become completely dissociated from their birth clouds. All that remains of the Pleiades' natal cloud, for example, are some wispy filaments that can be seen around a few of the stars.

As star clusters orbit the galactic center, the individual stars gradually drift apart and, eventually, lose their association with one another. In the case of the Sun, for example, it is now impossible for scientists to work out which stars were in the same cluster when it formed. Analysis has shown, however, that most of the stars that form the Big Dipper constellation are associated with one another and formed at the same time.

Curriculum Context

For many curricula, students should know that stars differ in size, color, chemical composition, surface gravity, and temperature, all of which affect the lifetime of the star, the spectrum of the radiation it emits, and its total energy.

Post-main Sequence

Throughout its entire main-sequence lifetime, only about 10 percent of the hydrogen in a star takes part in nuclear fusion. As the core runs out of hydrogen, fusion is confined to a shell around the inert core of helium. Because there are no energy-generating mechanisms at work in the core, it begins to contract, causing higher temperatures and pressures.

Core contraction is transmitted through the release of potential energy to the outer layers of the star. As these layers are bloated outward, the star puffs up greatly in size—often becoming 10–100 times larger in diameter. The temperature drops, however, and the star becomes redder. The star is now a red giant.

Further fusion

As the core continues to shrink, the temperature continues to rise. Eventually, the temperature rises high enough so that helium fusion begins in the core. The ignition is known as the helium flash, and the nuclear reaction employed is known as the triple alpha process. This involves two helium nuclei, often referred to as alpha particles, fusing together to form a radioactive beryllium isotope. If a third helium nucleus collides before the beryllium can decay, a stable carbon nucleus is produced. Sometimes, a fourth alpha particle takes part in the reaction and an oxygen nucleus is formed.

Stellar wind

A flow of neutral or charged gases from the upper atmosphere of a star. The gases may travel at speeds of hundreds of miles per second.

Carbon is produced until the helium is used up, and again the core becomes inert. In stars of similar mass to the Sun, this is as far as the nuclear fusion process goes. As the nuclear fusion processes subside and finally stop, the star begins to die. In low-mass stars, the outer gaseous layers are ejected by stellar wind processes. These may be the inevitable result of the pulsations that giant stars often suffer as they become Cepheid variable stars. The result of the mass loss, however, is to produce a planetary nebula. As the gas drifts outward from the central star, it is illuminated by the radiation that is still being released by the star. This radiation is absorbed by the gas in the shell of gas and re-emitted at visible wavelengths. The nebula gradually disperses and merges into the interstellar medium over a few hundred thousand years.

The central stars of planetary nebulas have been pulled into small, compact objects by the force of gravity. Sometimes they are white dwarfs—stars in which the density of matter is so great that the electrons can no longer exist in orbits around the nuclei. Instead, they are all compressed so that they try to occupy the lowest energy levels. The white dwarf cools gradually over the course of the next few billion years, until it finally becomes a body known as a black dwarf.

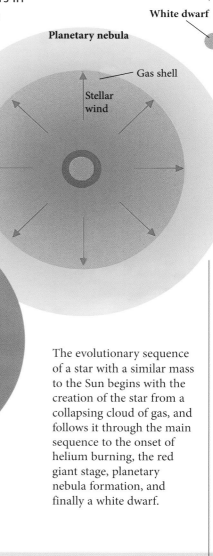

White dwarf

Planetary nebula

Gas shell

Stellar wind

Pulsating red giant

Helium core

Hydrogen-burning shell

Expanding envelope

Main sequence star

Hydrogen fusion in core

Protostar

The evolutionary sequence of a star with a similar mass to the Sun begins with the creation of the star from a collapsing cloud of gas, and follows it through the main sequence to the onset of helium burning, the red giant stage, planetary nebula formation, and finally a white dwarf.

Stellar Nucleosynthesis

The energy that makes a star shine comes from nuclear fusion reactions. In fact, the energy produced by nuclear fusion inside the star prevents it from collapsing under the crushing pull of its own gravity. As the radiation forces its way to the surface, it collides with atomic nuclei throughout the star, pushing them upward, resisting the downward pull of gravity.

Curriculum Context

For many curricula, students should know the evidence indicating that the color, brightness, and evolution of a star are determined by a balance between gravitational collapse and nuclear fusion.

Main sequence stars shine because they are fusing hydrogen into helium in their cores. However, this can happen in two different ways depending upon the mass of the main sequence star. The mass of a star is what determines the temperature at its center. In the case of a star like the Sun, that temperature is about 15 million Kelvin. At such temperatures, individual protons (hydrogen atom nuclei) collide to produce first deuterium and then tritium, both isotopes of hydrogen. In the most likely final stage of this reaction, two tritiums collide to produce one helium nucleus and two protons. This is known as the proton–proton chain.

Energy production in massive stars

All stars up to the mass of the Sun produce energy via the proton–proton chain. However, stars of greater mass than the Sun present a puzzle. Although their interiors can be perhaps three times hotter, they can be hundreds of times more luminous. The proton–proton chain cannot explain this prodigious output of energy.

The energy-producing reaction in these stars is called the carbon–nitrogen–oxygen reaction and requires the presence of carbon in the star's core. It is most efficient in younger, Population I stars that incorporate heavier elements created by a previous generation of stars. In these young hot stars, carbon acts as a catalyst. First, a proton collides with a carbon nucleus, creating an unstable isotope of nitrogen. This decays naturally into

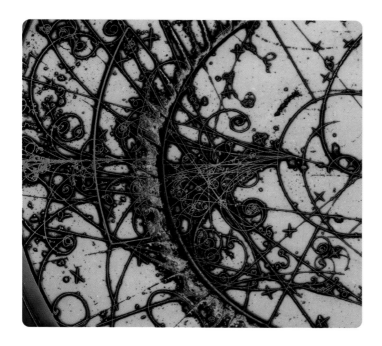

Physicists use particle accelerators to make particles collide with each other and see what happens. These collisions do not have enough energy to produce fusion, but they can produce sprays of different particles. This picture shows the tracks that particles leave in a type of detector called a bubble chamber.

a heavy isotope of carbon. Another proton collides with the heavy carbon turning it into a stable isotope of nitrogen. Then a third proton transforms the nitrogen into oxygen. Finally, a fourth proton joins with the oxygen and makes it split into a helium nucleus and the original, light carbon nucleus. Overall, the reaction creates helium out of four protons, just as the proton-proton chain did, but more energy is liberated because heavier nuclei are involved.

Heavier elements

In stars that have graduated beyond the main sequence, helium nuclei are the predominant reactants and they slowly build up heavier and heavier nuclei. Helium burning is responsible for creating carbon via the so-called triple alpha process, and oxygen is created by the addition of another helium nucleus to the other three. In low-mass stars, like the Sun, the reactions stop at oxygen but high-mass stars continue to build heavier and heavier atoms.

Isotopes

Atoms of the same element (i.e. with the same number of protons in the nucleus), but different numbers of neutrons.

Supernovae

A supernova is the explosion of a star, which begins with the collapse of the star's iron core. This sequence is sometimes bright enough to be seen on Earth even during daylight. The precise sequence of events that takes place in a supernova explosion has been investigated using sophisticated computer models.

Carbon fusion

In stars of more than seven solar masses, the inert carbon core is so massive that it collapses sufficiently to ignite carbon fusion. The temperature needed to ignite the carbon is in the region of several hundred million degrees. Carbon fusion produces magnesium, neon, sodium, silicon, sulfur, nickel, cobalt, and, finally, iron. Carbon fusion is usually complete within 1,000 years; neon and oxygen fusion takes place within a single year. The silicon burning, which produces the iron core, usually takes place within a day or two. Iron builds up in the core of the star and does not fuse into anything else. This is because the energy needed to fuse iron nuclei together is greater than the energy released in the fusion process. The iron accumulates in a mass at the center of the star. Eventually the core

Distance Measurement

The value of supernovae to astronomers is that they make excellent tools with which to measure distances in the Universe. The intensity of light changes as it spreads outward according to the inverse square law. This means that if you triple the distance from a light, its intensity drops by a factor of 9 (=3^2). If you know how bright the light is to start with, the amount it has dimmed can be used to work out how far away it is. Because supernovae all begin with the collapse of the iron core, the processes of collapse and explosion are similar in each one. The result is that all supernovae explode with roughly the same energy output and achieve roughly the same brightness. Thus, the observed brightness of a supernova can be compared to its theoretical brightness using the inverse square law, and the distance to the galaxy can be calculated.

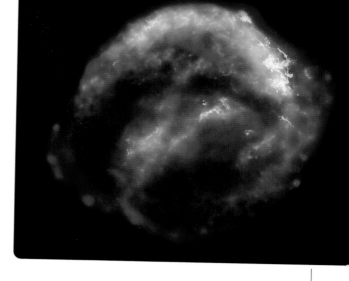

In 1604 the astronomer Johannes Kepler observed a "new star" in the sky, which was as bright as nearby planets. The "star" was the most recent supernova to be seen in the Milky Way galaxy. Today, the remnants of the event can be seen as a huge spherical cloud of hot gases and dust.

collapses even further, which has the same effect as knocking the foundations out from beneath a building. The overlying structure, in this case the rest of the star, begins to collapse downward. As the star crashes down upon itself, it releases so much energy that it explodes and virtually blows itself to bits. This is known as a supernova.

Core collapse

It takes just 80 milliseconds for the core to collapse from a diameter of 1250 miles (2,000 km) to 12.5 miles (20 km). This initial collapse is the beginning of a proto-neutron star. As the neutron star forms, electrons combine with protons, releasing a large quantity of neutrinos.

As the star continues to collapse, lighter material from above the core begins to rain down, reaching velocities of some 10,000 km/sec. This increases the density of material around the forming neutron star. As the neutron star reaches its most compact size, it stops collapsing and rebounds. This action strikes the overlying material and creates a shock wave. About a second after the onset of the core collapse, the shockwave has enough energy to expand explosively through the star. When it reach the star's surface, the outside Universe sees the star explode. In the cataclysmic nuclear furnace that is left behind, all the chemical elements heavier than iron can be made.

Neutron Stars and Pulsars

When the core of a massive star can no longer withstand the pressure caused by the downward pull of gravity, the stellar material collapses into a state called degenerate matter. Degenerate matter is matter in which the normal arrangement of atoms has broken down under the force of gravity because the weight of overlying material is so oppressive.

Degenerate matter

In baryon degenerate matter, the electrons—which usually orbit the atomic nuclei—have been forced into the nuclei, where they combine with the protons and form neutrons. As a result, the entire core of the star is composed of neutrons, tightly compressed.

Under these conditions the neutrons are still being tugged by gravity. But, according to Pauli's exclusion principle, in spite of the densely crowded conditions, no two identical particles may occupy the same quantum state (a set of conditions of location, spin, and velocity that may apply to a particle). In other words, two neutrons cannot be in the same place at the same time; it is physically impossible. So, just as the electrons did before them, the neutrons exert a pressure that resists further collapse, which would pull them even closer together.

Objects composed of neutrons are extremely compact. White dwarf stars, composed of electron-degenerate material, typically have a diameter similar to that of the Earth but contain more mass than the Sun. Neutron stars are even more extreme: they contain more mass than one-and-a-half Suns packed into a spherical region with a diameter of only 6.25 to 12.5 miles (10 to 20 km) —equivalent to the nuclear density of an atom. The star's ability to resist gravitational collapse by means of degeneracy pressure is limited by its mass. Up to 1.4

Neutron star

A very dense star remnant that is all that is left of a large star after a supernova.

times the mass of the Sun, the star can support itself by electron degeneracy pressure; this is called the Chandrasekhar limit. Beyond 1.4 solar masses, the matter collapses until it is halted by baryon degenerate pressure, which is effective up to the Oppenheimer–Volkoff limit of between three and five solar masses. This is the upper mass limit for a neutron star.

Electron degeneracy pressure

The outward pressure from electrons that cannot occupy the same energy levels, which resists the tendency of matter to collapse further during a supernova.

Pulsars

Neutron stars are left behind following supernova type II explosions. They are the collapsed cores of massive stars. Although their existence was predicted by theory in the 1930s, it was thought that they would be undetectable because of their small size. Then, in the

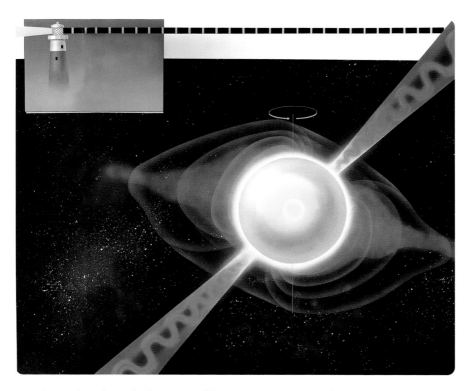

A pulsar is thought to flash on and off because it is rotating. This is known as the lighthouse model, because a lighthouse also seems to flash intermittently when in fact the light beam is rotating. Observation of pulsars shows that they emit radiation pulses at many different wavelengths. Pulses may vary in speed between pulsars; some are fast, and some slow.

1960s, a class of rapidly pulsating objects that became known as pulsars was discovered. It was soon shown that the only objects that could have such behavior were spinning neutron stars. They operate in a similar way to a lighthouse: although a lighthouse's the light appears to flash on and off, this is an illusion produced because the llight is rotating. In this same way, the beam of radiation is swept through space by a rotating pulsar. As it crosses our line of sight, we receive a pulse of radiation. Astronomers do not yet understand how this radiation is produced, nor why it is confined in such narrow beams.

Spinning up

After a supernova explosion, the neutron star is left spinning at high velocities. For instance, the pulsar in the center of the Crab nebula—which is the remains of a star that went supernova in 1054 CE—is spinning so fast that it flashes 30 times a second. The fastest pulsars are known as millisecond pulsars, and they can spin at hundreds of revolutions per second. These are old pulsars which have been "spun up" by accretion from nearby stars. This "spinning up" process is similar to the way in which material is funneled onto white dwarfs in binary star systems. Because of the properties of degenerate matter, the more mass a neutron star accumulates, the smaller it shrinks. The smaller a neutron star becomes, the faster it spins. Its magnetic field also increases by a factor of one billion (in proportion to its compressed surface area).

The process of spinning up a neutron star leads astrophysicists to expect an accretion disk to be formed around it. Around protostars, the accretion disk is the site of planet formation. A tentative discovery suggests that two planets have, indeed, formed around a pulsar, known as PSR1257+12. However, these "second generation" planets are not locations on which it is conceivable that life could develop.

Accretion

The process by which a massive object gathers in dust and gas from its surroundings, through gravitational attraction.

Black Holes

A collapsar is a star that has collapsed because nuclear fusion is no longer taking place within its core. Some collapsars become white dwarfs and neutron stars; others become black holes. The mass of the star determines whether it becomes a white dwarf, a neutron star, or a black hole.

What are black holes?

Black holes are objects that have exceeded a calculable limit for inert, non-energy producing material (about 3.2 times the mass of the Sun). This is known as the Oppenheimer–Volkoff limit. For stars with more mass than this, the matter in the star continues to collapse under the influence of gravity, and takes up less and less space. The smaller the star becomes, the greater the force of gravity at its surface. The greater the surface gravity, the greater the velocity needed to escape from the star. As the collapsing star gets smaller and smaller, the escape velocity rises until it is equal to the speed of light. When the escape velocity reaches this level, nothing can escape from the star—not even light—and it becomes a black hole. The star has then disappeared from the observable Universe, although some of its effects can still be detected.

The radius within which a star must be compressed before becoming a black hole is called the Schwarzschild radius. The more massive the star, the larger the Schwarzschild radius. It defines the region known as the event horizon—the edge of the black hole, where the escape velocity equals the speed of light. No one can ever know what takes place inside the boundaries of the event horizon. It is thought that the collapsing mass continues to shrink until it becomes a minuscule point of infinite density known as a singularity. Objects crossing the event horizon are believed to disappear into the singularity.

Binary systems

Because nothing can escape from a black hole, it is very difficult to discover one. Like white dwarf and neutron stars, black holes can exist in binary star systems. Gas from the companion star is gradually stripped away by the gravitational influence of the black hole, and funneled down into it. Because the star and the black hole rotate around one another, the material forms an accretion disk around the black hole. The material in this disk swirls around the black hole so fast that the friction between the molecules heats the gas until it begins to emit X rays; as it does, it loses energy and spirals into the black hole. The X rays can be detected on Earth, indicating a black hole.

Cygnus X-1

An example of a possible black hole is Cygnus X-1, an X-ray source in the constellation of Cygnus that orbits a blue supergiant star of between 20 and 30 solar masses. This massive star seems to be pulled gravitationally by an invisible companion with between 9 and 11 solar masses. This is probably a black hole, and it is slowly ripping the supergiant star apart. The outer layers of the star travel down into the black hole, spiraling into an accretion disk, which is so hot that it emits X-ray radiation. The X-ray emissions can be detected from the Earth.

KEY
1 Supergiant star
2 Black hole
3 Accretion disk
4 Hot spot

Open, Flat, or Closed

Every known object in the Universe is made of protons, neutrons, and electrons. Everything we see is visible because it emits or reflects photons of electromagnetic radiation. Are there other forms of matter that we cannot detect?

Dark matter

Astronomers now suspect that other forms of matter greatly outweigh normal, so-called baryonic, matter. Studies of galactic clusters suggest that the amount of matter in such clusters may exceed luminous material by ten to one. This means that 90 percent of the Universe is contained in forms of matter that are yet to be discovered. This invisible material is called dark matter. Two possible forms have been suggested: hot and cold. Hot dark matter may comprise particles such as neutrinos, which are extremely lightweight, travel at the speed of light, and barely interact with baryonic matter. Cold dark matter may be made up of the hypothetical particles sometimes referred to as Weakly Interacting Massive Particles (WIMPs). An alternative theory states that dark matter is normal nonluminous objects such as brown dwarfs and black holes.

The question of how much mass the Universe contains has a direct bearing on its eventual fate. It has been known since the 1920s that the Universe is expanding. Astronomers are now asking, will it ever stop expanding? The answer depends on how much mass there is in the Universe.

Curvature of the Universe

The presence of mass curves the spacetime continuum. On the very largest scale, the curvature of the Universe is determined by the average density of matter within it—that is, the average mass contained within a specific volume of space. The average density required to halt the expansion of the Universe—known as the

Curriculum Context

For most curricula, students should be aware that the presence of otherwise invisible matter can be inferred from the effect of its gravity on visible matter, and that the mass of the invisible matter in the Universe appears to be even greater than the mass of the visible.

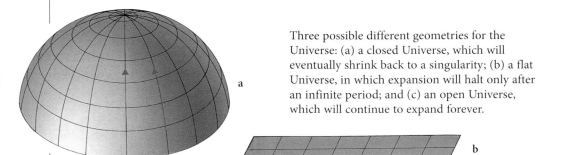

Three possible different geometries for the Universe: (a) a closed Universe, which will eventually shrink back to a singularity; (b) a flat Universe, in which expansion will halt only after an infinite period; and (c) an open Universe, which will continue to expand forever.

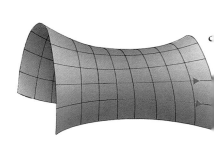

critical density—is only a few hydrogen atoms per cubic meter. The ratio of the average density of the Universe to the critical density is known as Ω (omega).

A Universe with Ω less than 1 will exist and expand forever and is known as an "open" Universe; its spacetime continuum has what astronomers call negative curvature. A Universe within which the expansion is halted through force of gravity is known as a "closed" Universe and spacetime has positive curvature. In a closed Universe the expansion of spacetime will eventually stop and then reverse, until the Universe disappears in a "Big Crunch."

A third possibility exists, known as the "flat" Universe. This occurs if there is just enough matter to halt the expansion, but only after an infinite period of time. Some estimates suggest that the average density of the Universe may equal the critical density. If so, the Universe is "flat" and will exist forever.

The Accelerating Universe

Until recently, astronomers believed that the Universe was in a state of decelerating expansion. The only question was whether the deceleration would halt that expansion or not. In 1997, however, a series of observations by two teams of astronomers, working independently, completely changed that view.

The astronomers were studying supernova explosions in the distant Universe. These celestial bursts of energy shine—briefly—with the intensity of a billion Suns and as a result become beacons that astronomers can use to study the Universe on its largest scales.

The supernovae both groups of astronomers observed were called type I supernovae, which occur when a white dwarf star accumulates material from a red giant companion and then eventually explodes. Such supernovae always explode with a similar brightness (see page 62). By measuring the apparent brightness of the supernova from Earth, astronomers can determine its distance from us, based upon the fact that light becomes dimmed the farther it travels.

Red shift measurements

Another way of determining the distance to a faraway object is to measure the red shift of the light coming from it. The farther away an object is in space, the greater its red shift. The light of the supernova suffers a red shift because of the expansion of the Universe.

When the two teams of astronomers calculated how far away a number of supernovae were, using both red shift and brightness calculations, they found that the figures did not add up. The supernovae were fainter than expected by about 25 percent. The best explanation the teams could find for this data was that the expansion of the Universe had accelerated

Red shift

A Doppler shift in the wavelength of light toward longer wavelengths produced when luminous objects (such as distant galaxies) are moving rapidly away from the observer.

Curriculum Context

For many curricula, students should know how the red shift from distant galaxies and the cosmic background radiation provide evidence for the Big Bang theory.

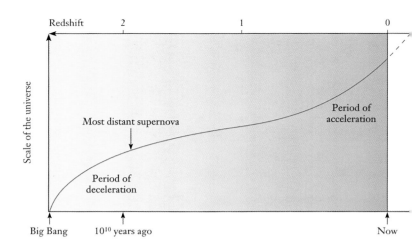

This graph shows how astronomers think the Universe has expanded since the Big Bang. Initially, expansion decelerated because of the braking effect of gravity. Then, however, a new force, dubbed dark energy, took over, and has caused expansion to accelerate.

since the supernovae took place (this happened about 5 billion years ago).

Dark energy

To explain the accelerated expansion of the Universe, astronomers have suggested the existence of an exotic form of energy known as dark energy. Matter, which produces gravity, can only cause attraction and so can only decelerate the Universe. Dark energy, however, has the opposite effect. Albert Einstein (1879–1955) introduced a term into his equation of general relativity that allowed for dark energy to exist. This term is called the cosmological constant, but Einstein later abandoned it, calling it his "greatest mistake."

The supernovae observations that imply an accelerating Universe have sparked a resurgence of interest in the cosmological constant. However it seems that a simple constant term that applies across the Universe for all time is not the best way to explain what is happening. Instead, the quantity of vacuum energy seems to have altered with time in such a way that, initially after inflation, the Universe was in a state of decelerating expansion but, about six or seven billion years ago, the Universe changed and dark energy took over, causing the cosmos to accelerate.

Accretion of the Planets

About 4.6 billion years ago, one of several regions in a giant cloud of dust and gas in the Milky Way began to collapse and rotate under the effects of gravity. This cloud, called the solar nebula, had a diameter somewhat larger than the orbit of Pluto. It was the beginning of the Solar System, of which Earth is a part.

After about 100 million years, the central mass of this nebula had grown large enough to become a protostar. The protostar started to spin rapidly, and the gas and dust cloud around it flattened into a slowly rotating disk. This disk gradually evolved into the Sun's family of planets and moons.

Planetesimals

Most accounts of the emergence of the planets from the original solar nebula describe the growth of large planets from much smaller bodies by a process of accretion, as their orbits drew them into collisions, or as the force of gravity sucked smaller bodies toward larger ones. Most scientists now think that the planets accreted from larger original bodies, known as planetesimals, or protoplanets. The building blocks of the modern planets certainly include much larger fragments than dust particles, since huge impact basins scar the oldest surfaces of most solid bodies in the Solar System. Some of these must have been produced by the impact of bodies over half a mile (1 kilometer) in diameter.

Accretion of material

Collisions between fast-moving particles, both large and small, were surely very frequent within the solar nebula. During some collisions one fragment may have been shattered completely or even vaporized; during others—particularly collisions involving one large body and another much smaller—part of the smaller body

Protostar
A hot ball of gas that has not yet grown large enough or hot enough for fusion to begin in its core.

Curriculum Context

For many curricula, students should know that evidence from Earth and Moon rocks indicates that the Solar System was formed from a nebular cloud of dust and gas approximately 4.6 billion years ago.

a

b

may have become embedded inside the former, increasing its mass. In this way, larger bodies grew at the expense of smaller ones. Exactly how the fragments stuck together (accreted) is not entirely understood, but the production of a dusty soil-like surface known as a regolith is thought to have assisted the process.

The planetesimals warm

Each collision caused the enormous energy associated with rapid movement to be transferred instantly from one particle to the other. Some of this kinetic energy was converted into thermal energy, thus generating intense heat. When the fragments were small, this heat was soon lost to space, but for larger pieces, heat gradually accumulated deep inside. Consequently the larger planetesimals slowly heated up as they grew.

Three distinct types of planet emerged, associated with these three regions of the early nebula. In the hot central regions, the first solid condensates would have been iron-bearing silicates and metal oxides. Here, small, rocky planets formed. Further out, where it was cooler, ices and liquids of carbon compounds, water and oxygen collected, surrounded by layers of gas.

c

How the planets formed from the solar nebula. (a) A protostar
begins to form in the center of the rotating cloud of gas and dust.
(b) As the protostar forms it begins to spin quickly, and the dust
and gas around it forms a flattened disk. (c) Planetesimals form,
then accrete more material until they reach the size of the planets
we see today.

Here Jupiter and Saturn, the giant gas planets, formed.
The lightest constituents, such as hydrogen and
helium, collected in the coldest regions of the nebula.
Here the giant ice planets formed. All these different
planets—together with millions of smaller bodies such
as asteroids, meteoroids, and comets—formed within
the solar nebula as it cooled and evolved into its
present stable configuration.

Orbits

Each planet describes a mildly elliptical orbit around
the Sun, while the planetary orbits all lie in the plane of
the original solar nebula. The mutual gravitational
attraction of the Sun and planets—due to their various
masses—keeps the Solar System together.

Large and Small Planets

At first the solar nebula was probably well mixed, reached a temperature approaching 3600°F (2000°C), and was mainly gaseous. As it cooled, the nebula separated into materials that were physically and chemically unlike. Temperatures were highest close to the proto-Sun, and the first solid particles to form there were made from refractory elements such as tungsten, aluminum, and calcium, forming oxides.

Curriculum Context

For many curricula, students need to know the role of gravity in forming and maintaining the shapes of planets, stars, and the Solar System.

As further cooling occurred, these reacted with gases in the nebula to form silicates. The inner planets, which formed close to the Sun, are largely composed of silicate minerals (rocks) rich in elements such as magnesium, aluminum, calcium, and iron, and are therefore relatively dense. Many meteorites and asteroids are made from these minerals.

Farther from the Sun, where the nebular temperatures were around 122°F (50°C), compounds rich in carbon would have crystallized out. Water ice may have existed as snowflakes and become incorporated into the solids that formed. In more distant regions, at even lower temperatures, volatile (gaseous) elements such as argon, and compounds such as ammonia and methane would have crystallized. The lightest elements, hydrogen and helium, probably never condensed at all. The volatile elements were far more abundant than the refractory (solid) ones: the latter probably accounted for a mere 0.5 percent of the total mass of the nebula.

Planetary formation

Once planets had begun to condense, growth accelerated, with very rapid accretion of carbonaceous materials, volatile-rich silicates, and ices of compounds such as water, methane, and ammonia. The abundance of icy material partly explains the large masses of Jupiter, Saturn, Uranus, and Neptune. More of this cold volatile matter formed comets—smaller icy bodies that accumulated even farther from the Sun.

Timing of changes

The speed of these developments can be estimated from meteorites that contain radioactive isotopes. These decay to other isotopes, at a rate referred to as the half-life of the isotope. One of the isotopes found in them is Al-26 (an isotope of aluminum with one less neutron than normal in the nuceus): its half-life is 720,000 years. Another is the iodine isotope I-128 (half-life 16 million years). Neither of these is native to the Solar System and must have come from distant supernova stars. They were captured by the solar nebula and locked into meteorites that formed in the early Solar System. This proves that accretion must have been quick: perhaps a few million years after the emergence of the proto-Sun.

Radioactive isotopes

Atoms with unstable nuclei that decay (break down) by release of either particles or energy from the nucleus. The release of nuclear material is termed radioactivity.

Drawn to scale, the largest of the planets, Jupiter, could swallow up over 1300 Earths. The outer group of large planets are gaseous or icy, while the inner group are rocky. Pluto, which used to be considered the outermost planet, was formally reclassified in 2006 by the International Astronomical Union. It is one of several similar dwarf planets now known as Trans-Neptunian objects.

Planets and their Orbits

Energy from the Sun bathes its attendant family of planets, which travel in almost circular orbits around it. Earth is one of an inner group of four rocky planets, the others being Mercury, Venus, and Mars. Farther out are four much larger bodies, two of which (Jupiter and Saturn) are composed primarily of gas, and two (Uranus and Neptune) mainly of ice. The planets shine in the reflected sunlight; they do not generate light by nuclear reactions.

Curriculum Context

For most curricula, students should know that stars are the source of light for all bright objects in outer space and that the Moon and planets shine by reflected sunlight, not by their own light.

Solar System composition

Small rocky asteroids are concentrated in orbits between those of Mars and Jupiter. Many such objects crashed into the solid surfaces of the planets during the early years of the Solar System, forming impact craters and large basins. Beyond Neptune, Pluto (once the ninth planet) and a number of other dwarf planets comprise the Trans-Neptunian objects. Many of the planets have rock and ice moons, or orbiting systems of rings.

The Sun's family is completed by icy comets, which originated in the far reaches of the Solar System and have mainly parabolic orbits. Many come close to the Earth and occasionally become spectacular objects in the night sky. Meteors are other small particles that often stray close to the Earth.

Planetary motion

In 1609 the astronomer Johannes Kepler discovered that the planets circled the Sun in elliptical, rather than circular, orbits and that the Sun occupied one focus of each ellipse. This discovery was formulated into his laws of planetary motion. When closest to the Sun, a planet or other body is said to be at perihelion; at its most distant, it is at aphelion. The difference in the two measures is described as the eccentricity, a measure of how elliptical (oval) an orbit is. However, with the exception of Mercury, most planetary orbits are nearly circular.

The minimum distance to the Sun of the innermost planet, Mercury, is 35.9 million miles (57.9 million km), while the maximum distance of the outermost planet (Neptune) is 2.794 billion miles (4.497 billion kilometers). The mean radius of the Earth's orbit is 92.9 million miles (149.6 million km). This distance is used frequently by astronomers as a convenient unit of measurement, known as the astronomical unit (AU).

Except for Mercury, Pluto, and Charon, the planetary orbits all lie in the same plane, due to the gravitational attraction exerted by the Sun. Because the Sun and most of the planets share this orbital plane, each moves against the star background along the same path, known as the ecliptic. This passes through the twelve constellations of the zodiac. Material that did not get swept up into major bodies does not always follow this pattern, and many comets have orbits highly inclined to the plane.

Planetary Data

Planet	Mean distance from Sun (x 10^6 miles)	Equatorial diameter (miles)	Sidereal period (days)	Equatorial rotation (hr)	Mass (lb)
Mercury	4.92	3031	87.97	1407.60	7.27×10^{23}
Venus	67.23	7464	224.70	5832.00	10.71×10^{24}
Earth	92.96	7922	365.26	23.93	13.13×10^{24}
Mars	141.64	4217	686.98	24.62	14.12×10^{23}
Jupiter	483.63	88,846	4332.71	9.80	4.18×10^{27}
Saturn	886.68	74,898	10,759.50	10.60	12.50×10^{26}
Uranus	1783.95	31,763	30,685.00	17.90	19.11×10^{25}
Neptune	2794.35	30,758	60,190.00	19.20	2.25×10^{26}

Eccentricity is the degree to which an orbit departs from circularity. Mercury has the most eccentric orbit, and Venus the least. The rotational axes are inclined at various angles to the orbital plane. Jupiter has a small axial inclination; Saturn and Neptune are slightly more inclined than the Earth; and the axis of Uranus is almost in the orbital plane. Pluto's orbit is also shown, although it is no longer considered to be a planet.

Planetary rotation

Individual planets rotate on axes that have varying inclinations with respect to the plane of the ecliptic—a property known as obliquity. Thus the Earth's rotational axis is inclined at 23.4°, and that of Jupiter is 3.2°. Most strange of all is Uranus, which is tilted on its side and has an axial inclination of 97.9°. The varying obliquities may be related to ancient collisions, which may also have affected the ultimate distances of the planets from the Sun. Indeed, the rotation of Venus, which is unusual in that it rotates the opposite way to the Earth, could be due to such an event.

The inclination of planets' rotational axes is not fixed; long-term changes give rise to the phenomenon of precession, or wobbling of the axis. Today, for instance, the axis of Mars is inclined at 25° to the plane of its orbit. But this has not always been so. It is known that the axis "wobbles" slightly, like a child's spinning top, completing one cycle every 175,000 years. The axis of its orbit also changes slowly, precessing once every 72,000 years. Similar changes also affect the Earth. In both cases, such changes give rise to rapidly changing climatic patterns.

25°

26.7°

97.9°

29.6°

52

Pluto

Uranus

Neptune

ars

Jupiter

Saturn

Solstices and equinoxes

Seen from the Earth, the Sun moves around the sky once a year, reaching its northernmost point around June 22 (summer solstice) and its southernmost point around December 22 (winter solstice) in the northern hemisphere. During the northern summer the North Pole is tilted toward the Sun. It is summer in northern latitudes, while southern latitudes experience winter. The reverse occurs during the northern winter. During the year, the Sun crosses the celestial equator twice: at the vernal equinox (around March 22) and at the autumnal equinox (around September 22). At these times, day and night are of equal length in both hemispheres. Because the difference between perihelion and aphelion for the Earth is only 3 million miles (5 million km), this has only a modest influence upon the seasons. Mars also has seasons.

Earth and Moon

The Moon is unusually large in relation to its planetary neighbor, with a diameter more than a quarter that of the Earth. The two are often seen as a double planet system, orbiting around a common point deep within the Earth. The strong gravitational pull of the Moon upon the Earth, and on its oceans in particular, gives rise to twice-daily tides.

The Moon orbits the Earth at a mean distance of 238,850 miles (384,392 kilometers). It takes one month to complete each revolution and the same period to rotate once on its axis. As a result it directs the same face toward the Earth at all times, and the far side is never seen from Earth. The Moon's monthly phases are dependent on the angles between the Earth, Sun, and Moon at different times.

The mean density of the Moon is significantly less than that of the Earth. Since much of the Earth's high average density derives from the heavy material in its core, this suggests that, unlike Earth, the Moon does not have a large dense core.

The Moon's surface

The Moon's surface shows the results of considerable cratering. Since the Moon has no atmosphere and apparently has never had one, its surface was afforded no protection from attack by planetesimals. As a result, the lunar surface is pockmarked with impact craters and basins. The older a surface is, the more craters it has. The most heavily cratered regions, the highlands, have a higher albedo (reflect light more brightly) and lie at a higher level than the darker regions known as "seas" or maria. The reflectivity of the former is due to the light-colored rock anorthosite, which is rich in the elements calcium and aluminum and forms the ancient crust. Rock samples from the highlands have been

Planetesimals

Small solid celestial bodies that are thought to have been the "seeds" of the planets.

shown to be some 4.5 billion years old, older than any known rocks from the Earth's crust. These ancient rocks suffered severe bombardment by planetesimals until 4 billion years ago.

The maria are younger and have smoother surfaces. They are made from the volcanic rock basalt. This rock rose from inside the Moon and flowed out as lava, which filled several huge impact basins, such as Mare Imbrium. This took place in phases between 3.9 and 3 billion years ago, which implies that the interior of the Moon was hot for at least this long.

Formation of the Moon

At one time it was believed that the Moon derived from the Earth, somehow ejected from the Pacific, but this idea is now discounted. Modern research suggests that soon after the Earth's core had formed, a massive celestial object gave the Earth a glancing blow. This object was vaporized, and the Moon formed largely from its mantle.

Curriculum Context

For many curricula, students should know that various types of exploratory missions have yielded much information about the reflectivity, structure, and composition of the Moon and the planets.

Apollo 17 astronaut Harrison H. Schmitt examines a large boulder in the highland regions of the Moon. Samples of Moon rock brought back to Earth have revealed a great deal about the Moon's geological history.

Inner Planets

Mercury, Venus, Earth, and Mars, the four inner or "terrestrial" planets, accreted close to the proto-Sun, where temperatures in the nebula were high and only dense silicate materials were condensing. In consequence they all have high mean densities, ranging from 1.9 ounces per cubic inch (3.3 g/cm^3) for Mars to 3.2 ounces per cubic inch (5.5 g/cm^3) for Earth. All have a crust (surface layers) and mantle (inner solid layers) made from silicate rocks, and a denser core which is rich in iron.

Mercury

Mercury orbits the Sun at a mean distance of 36.0 million miles (57.9 million km), but is peculiar in that it has a more elliptical orbit than most planets, while its orbit is inclined to the ecliptic plane at 7.2°—a greater inclination than any planet except Uranus. Mercury is particularly dense for its size, and has a large core that extends to three-quarters of the radius. It has a weak magnetic field, which suggests that at least a part of the core is still fluid.

Compressional fault scarp

A scarp (cliff or steep slope) produced when compressional forces cause rocks to fault or fracture, and one side of the fracture becomes raised above the other.

The surface of Mercury is pockmarked with impact craters and one huge basin—the Caloris Basin—that is 800 miles (1300 km) across. It was first photographed in detail by the space probe *Mariner 10* in 1974. Between the craters are smoother plains, presumably of volcanic origin. Compressional fault scarps 3000 feet (*ca.* 1000 meters) high cross the surface. These faults indicate that the planet underwent a contraction of about 1.25 to 2.5 miles (2–4 km), which probably occurred about four billion years ago.

Mercury's relatively high density and unusually large core size are generally explained by a collision that is thought to have occurred long ago with a body of about one-fifth the planet's mass. This would have stripped away most of the planet's mantle.

Venus

Venus is comparable with Earth in terms of size, mass, and density, but has a dense carbon dioxide atmosphere, a slow retrograde rotation (its day is 243 Earth days), and no moon. The atmosphere prevents heat from escaping and generates a greenhouse effect; surface temperatures can reach 932°F (500°C).

The *Magellan* space probe, which took radar images of the planet, revealed fine details of the Venusian surface. It is dominated by volcanic plains on which are found hundreds of circular structures called coronae, different kinds of volcanoes, domes, and impact craters. The relatively small number of impact craters implies that the age of much of the surface is relatively young (450–500 million years).

Venus also has highland regions of complex structure. One of these, Ishtar Terra, has surrounding mountains apparently formed by compressional forces; at Maxwell Montes they rise to heights of more than 7 miles (11 km). East of Maxwell, and elsewhere on the

Most of the data for this view of the surface of Venus was collected over a period of years by the *Magellan* space probe. The image has been processed by computer and color-coded to show elevation.

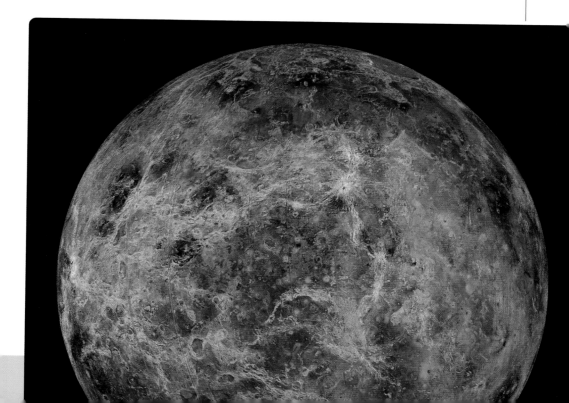

planet, are intricately grooved regions called tesserae, which bear witness to past movements of the crust.

Soviet *Venera* space probes landed on Venus during the 1970s, photographing the blocky surface and analyzing the surface rocks. The probes showed that volcanoes played a dominant role in Venus's history.

Mars

Mars has an orbit beyond the Earth's (its mean distance from the Sun is 141.6 miles, 227.9 million km). It is only half as big as Earth (diameter 4217 miles, 6787 km) and considerably less dense (2.3 ounces per cubic inch, 3.9 g/cm^3). The surface temperature is low, ranging between −220 and +68°F (−140 and +20°C); liquid water cannot exist on its surface, owing to the low temperatures and an atmospheric pressure only a hundredth that of Earth. The thin atmosphere is largely carbon dioxide. This, together with some water vapor, freezes at the poles, and gives rise to polar "ice" caps, which expand and contract with the seasons.

Lithosphere

The rocky outermost layer of a planet, consisting of the crust and the upper mantle.

North of a boundary inclined at about 28° to the equator, the surface of Mars consists of volcanic plains and huge shield volcanoes, many concentrated on a massive swelling in the lithosphere known as the Tharsis Bulge. A spectacular equatorial canyon system, Valles Marineris, runs eastward from this bulge.

Volatiles

Elements and molecules with low boiling points, which normally exist in gaseous form.

The southern latitudes are heavily cratered by impacts, and are older than the northern plains. Extensive valley networks and massive outflow channels have developed there, bearing witness to the past activity of running water. Most of the original volatiles probably remain, but they are locked in the porous rock of the surface layer. This implies that the planet's atmosphere has probably changed in the course of its history.

Life on Mars?

Mars has long been an object of curiosity to those who wonder whether there could be extraterrestrial life. During the 1970s, NASA sent two space probes, each consisting of an orbiter and lander, to search for life on Mars. *Viking 1* and *Viking 2* landed in 1976, on plains called Utopia Planitia and Chryse Planitia. Together with a battery of other scientific instruments and experiments, each probe carried three experiments that were designed to search for Martian microbes.

Viking conclusions

After extensive tests and evaluations of the results, the general conclusion was that the *Viking* probes failed to detect life. This does not mean Mars is entirely dead but it is certain that there is no widespread ecosystem as there is on Earth. That would have been noticeable from orbit, if not from our planet. In fact, earlier astronomers who looked at Mars through telescopes wondered whether the dark markings on the surface were oceans. We now know that is not the case. However, perhaps Martian life exists in certain sheltered environments, such as underground or under the polar ice sheets.

The discovery of earthly microbes living in Antarctica under conditions not dissimilar to those that may be found at the Martian poles, supports this hope that life may exist in places. For example, there are particularly hardy single-celled creatures in Antarctica, estimated to be able to live for 10,000 years on a single molecule of water!

Life in the past?

Just because there is no widespread life on Mars today does not mean that life might not have begun on the planet, billions of years ago. There is abundant geological evidence that Mars was once a very

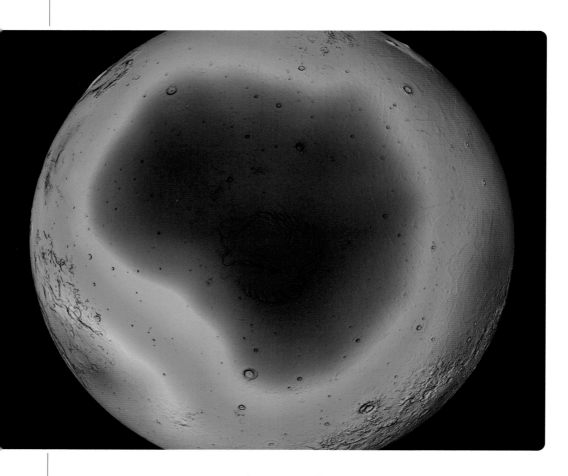

Mars today is essentially a desert planet, but evidence from the Mars *Odyssey* orbiter shows the presence of significant amounts of water (as ice) in Martian soils. The highest concentrations are at the poles. This false-colour image shows the north pole in summer. The blue indicates high levels of water ice in the soil.

different planet, perhaps much warmer and wetter than it is today. Mars would have been seeded with organic molecules from colliding comets, as was Earth. The now extinct Martian volcanoes must have been active. Life may have started on Mars around the same time it did on Earth, 3.8 billion years ago.

Adding to the controversy about whether Mars was once alive and might still be today, is a meteorite found in the Allen Hills region of Antarctica during 1984. It is called ALH84001 and is similar to the so-called SNC meteorites (named after the first three groups found, Shergotty, Nakhla, and Chassigny), which have been proven to come from Mars. Inside ALH84001 were a number of chemical substances. Some of them proved that the rock had been subjected to warm, running water and others could have been produced by the presence of life. Also found inside were tubular structures that resembled fossilized bacteria on Earth. Some scientists think that these are indeed the fossil evidence of past Martian life; others are strongly opposed to that conclusion.

Proponents of life on Mars were encouraged by images of Mars taken by *Mars Global Surveyor*, which revealed features that appeared to be relatively recent water gullies. Such data increases the hope that large quantities of water may reside in aquifers below the surface of the planet.

Mars Missions

There have been more unmanned space missions to Mars than to any other planet. Currently three space probes are orbiting Mars and three vehicles are based on the surface. All these missions have found evidence for the existence of water on Mars, both in the past and today. The Mars *Odyssey* orbiter, for example, found evidence that oceans covered about one-third of Mars in the past. Most recently, the Mars *Phoenix* spacecraft, which touched down on the northern plains of Mars in 2008, actually found water ice in a soil sample taken from the Martian surface.

Distant Companions

Jupiter, Saturn, Uranus, and Neptune are collectively called the Jovian planets because the other planets are similar in many respects to Jupiter, which dominates the group. There are, however, significant differences between the Jupiter–Saturn pair and the Uranus–Neptune pair.

Jupiter

Jupiter, the largest planet, has a mass 318 times that of Earth, yet its mean density (0.77 ounces per cubic inch, 1.33 g cm^{-3}) is only one-quarter of the Earth's—similar to that of the Sun. This giant world is composed mainly of hydrogen and helium which, in the outer cloud layers and down to a depth of over 600 miles (1000 km), occur as gas. Below this, gas gives way to liquid hydrogen for a further 12,500 miles (20,000 km), where the pressure is so great that the hydrogen behaves like a metal. There is believed to be a dense rocky core of about 10 to 30 Earth masses at the center.

Despite its huge size, Jupiter has the shortest rotation period of all the planets, spinning once every 9 hours 50 minutes, a phenomenon that causes the equatorial regions to bulge significantly. Parallel bands of light and dark clouds can be seen, as well as one semipermanent atmospheric feature, the Great Red Spot, a vast revolving weather system. The light zones comprise cold, high-altitude ammonia-ice clouds, while the darker belts represent lower-level clouds made from various hydrogen compounds.

Jupiter

Saturn

Saturn has a diameter nine times that of Earth and a composition and structure similar to that of Jupiter. Most distinctive is its magnificent ring system, which has a diameter of 170,000 miles (273,000 km). This was explored by the *Voyager* spacecraft in 1979 and shown to consist of billions of small rock and ice particles, ranging in size from dust to pieces the dimensions of a house. Small moons (called shepherd moons) orbit within the system, helping to maintain the gaps between the component rings. The *Cassini* space probe discovered many more details of the rings during a four-year period orbiting Saturn from 2004.

Uranus and Neptune

Uranus, with a diameter four times that of Earth, was the first planet to be discovered by telescope. Like Saturn and Jupiter, it has a hydrogen-rich atmosphere. However, it has a far greater proportion of ices (in particular, water ice and ammonia) than these two planets. Uranus has a ring system like Saturn, but much simpler and less obvious. The ring system was first discovered in 1977, and further rings were found by the *Voyager 2* space probe in 1986, and by the Hubble Space Telescope between 2003 and 2005.

Neptune, though somewhat larger and denser than Uranus, is similar. Prominent cloud bands and a Great Dark Spot characterize its bluish disk. It is likely that beneath the outer gaseous envelopes of both worlds—which contain much methane—there is a

Jupiter, the innermost of the outer group of planets, is a gas giant, like its companion Saturn. Jupiter's diameter is a little more than one-tenth that of the Sun, but its mass is one-thousandth that of the Sun. The next pair of planets, Uranus and Neptune, are gas-and-ice giants.

Saturn

Uranus

Neptune

deep layer of slushy ice surrounding a denser rocky-metallic core.

The giant planets probably formed cores of the more refractory elements very quickly and then collected their gaseous envelopes by accretion. The large mass of Jupiter may be due to its position near the "snow line", the point where water and other volatiles collected and cooled as intense solar activity cleared regions closer to the Sun of lighter elements.

Many moons

Each of the giant planets has many moons: Jupiter has at least 16; Saturn 18; Uranus 15; and Neptune 8. The largest of Neptune's moons, Triton, is the only large moon to have a retrograde orbit, while Saturn's giant moon, Titan, has a deep atmosphere. The two *Voyager* spacecraft passed close by many of these worlds, revealing active sulfur–silicate volcanism on Jupiter's moon, Io; impact cratering and tectonic deformations on many other moons; huge fault scarps, and peculiar icy volcanism known as cryovolcanism on Triton. In 2004 the probe *Huygens*, released from the *Cassini* spacecraft, landed on the surface of Saturn's moon Titan and sent back pictures suggesting the presence of water ice. Evidence from the *Galileo* and *Voyager* space probes suggests that Europa, one of Jupiter's largest moons, has a body of liquid water beneath its frozen surface.

Pluto and the Trans-Neptunian objects

Pluto and its companion Charon were at one time considered to be planets. However, in 2006 the International Astronomical Union decided to change Pluto's status to that of a dwarf planet. This was partly because several similar-sized objects have now been discovered, including Eris, which is larger than Pluto.

Accretion

The capture of gas, dust, and other material by a planet, star, or other massive body. The material is attracted to the surface by gravitational forces.

Retrograde orbit

An orbit that goes "backward," i.e. in the opposite direction to that of other planets, moons, or satellites.

Moons of the Outer Planets

The four gas giants of the outer Solar System—Jupiter, Saturn, Uranus, and Neptune—each have a fascinating collection of moons. During the late 1990s and the early 2000s, the *Galileo* space probe made observations in and around Jupiter, showing its moons in great detail and gathering a lot of information about them. In early 2005 the *Cassini* spacecraft dropped a probe, *Huygens*, onto Saturn's moon Titan.

Many outer Solar System moons should be considered worlds in their own right. For example, Ganymede (around Jupiter) is the largest moon in the Solar System, larger than the planet Mercury.

Io

Another moon of Jupiter, Io, is the most volcanically active body in the Solar System. Every year, Io erupts about 100 times the amount of lava that the Earth does. Lava makes Io spectacularly colourful. Mostly, these colors are produced by the element sulfur. Lava that has been squirted out through volcanic vents is red. Eventually, the lava turns yellow. Jupiter's powerful gravitational field is the cause of Io's intense volcanic activity. It raises enormous tides, squeezing the moon and heating the interior. The heat is then expelled through the volcanoes.

Europa

Another large moon of Jupiter, Europa, is one of the most interesting places in the Solar System. The tidal forces of Jupiter have produced a global ocean under a thick ice crust, in places over 6 miles (10 km) thick. The ocean is thought to be over 60 miles (100 km) deep. There is more probably more water on Europa than on Earth. Many now wonder whether simple microbes live in these oceans. The fourth large moon of Jupiter, Callisto, may also have a subsurface ocean.

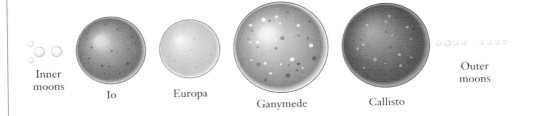

Inner moons   Io   Europa   Ganymede   Callisto   Outer moons

Titan

The second largest moon in the Solar System, Titan is known to have a dense atmosphere that is thought to be broadly similar to the probable atmosphere around Earth 4 billion years ago, before the birth of life. The *Huygens* probe sampled the thick atmosphere, and found that it was an orange smog made mainly of nitrogen, methane, and argon.

The moons of Uranus and Neptune are generally small and contain varying mixtures of rock and ice. No plans exist to explore them further.

The interiors of Jupiter's moons Io and Europa show that both moons possess a dense core, composed of metals, surrounded by a rocky mantle. In the case of Io, it then has a thin crust covered in molten lava. Europa has a layer of liquid water beneath a crust of water ice.

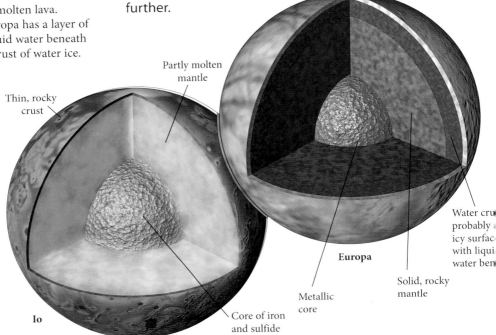

Partly molten mantle

Thin, rocky crust

Io

Core of iron and sulfide

Metallic core

Solid, rocky mantle

Europa

Water cru— probably — icy surfac— with liqui— water ben—

Bits and Pieces

Millions of small bodies, as well as the eight planets of the Solar System, are in orbit around the Sun. Among these bodies, the asteroids, or "minor planets", form a prominent group. Most orbit the Sun between Jupiter and Mars, but some have paths that cross the orbit of the Earth.

The largest asteroid, called Ceres, was discovered by the Italian astronomer Giuseppe Piazzi (1746–1826) in 1801; it measures 623 miles (1003 kilometers) across. The smallest yet found (6344P-L) is a mere 650 feet (200 m) in diameter. It is believed that there are at least a million asteroids larger than about 1 mile (*ca.* 1.6 km) across. Some have very irregular shapes, for example the Manhattan-sized meteorite Eros, which was visited by the space probe *NEAR*.

Asteroid fragmentation

Asteroids originally resembled the other nebular objects that accreted to form planets. But before groups of asteroids could stick together to form large bodies, they were affected by the gravitational pull of the Sun and the planets, and were sent into tilted, elongated orbits. These irregular orbits brought them into collision with one another so that fragmentation continued. This breakup of asteroids continues to occur, though less strongly, to the present.

The powerful gravitational influence of Jupiter as it grew must have inhibited the growth of a major planet in the position where the main asteroid belt now exists. Its gravitational effects would have sent some particles flying toward the planets (sometimes colliding with them and forming craters), and others out of the Solar System completely. Those smaller particles that were pushed into Earth-crossing trajectories are known as meteoroids.

Technicians at Kennedy Space Center work on the *Dawn* space probe. Launched in 2007, *Dawn*'s mission is to visit the largest asteroids, Ceres and Vesta. It will reach Vesta between 2011 and 2012, and Ceres in 2015.

Composition

When viewed through a telescope, many asteroids show changes in brightness. In large part this is due to their irregular shape, but some have different reflectivity from one side to the other, which suggests they have a variable composition. The most abundant types of asteroid are type C or carbonaceous class. These bodies are darker than coal and tend to be found in the outer regions of the belt. S-type bodies are silica-rich, of intermediate albedo (reflectivity), and dominate the mid-regions of the belt, while the M class have moderate albedos and are metallic. M-class asteroids probably represent the metal-rich cores of larger differentiated parent asteroids that broke up.

Meteorite

A meteoroid (an asteroid on an Earth-crossing trajectory) that reaches the Earth's surface.

Meteorites

Meteoroids are even more abundant than asteroids and show a similar range in chemistry. When they come under the influence of terrestrial gravity and enter the Earth's atmosphere, the resulting friction causes them to heat up, and a fireball or shooting star may be seen. Most such bodies fragment in the atmosphere, but pieces of larger ones may reach the

Earth's surface, providing planetary scientists with invaluable rock samples that give us concrete geochemical data about the early Solar System.

Classifying meteorites

Meteorites are traditionally categorized as stones, irons, or stony-irons—distinctions comparable with those of the asteroid groups. A more meaningful distinction can be made between "differentiated" and "undifferentiated" types. In the undifferentiated group are the chondrites, which contain chemical elements in similar proportions to the solar atmosphere. When these are dated, they reveal their ages to be about 4.5 billion years, representing some of the most primitive Solar System material known to modern science. The differentiated types have undergone chemical changes and are considered the products of melting and separation of more primitive planetary matter.

A few younger objects, known as SNC meteorites, resemble the surface of Mars and may have come from an impact with that planet.

Chondrites contain high-temperature aluminum-rich inclusions, volatile materials, and peculiar spherical particles called chondrules, which are the products of primordial melting. From the presence of these ingredients, it is evident that the material that comprised the solar nebula was well mixed at the time of planet accretion.

Meteorite orbits

Precise photography of some meteorites allows their orbits to be calculated and indicates that these orbits closely resemble those of Earth-crossing asteroids (such as Apollo and Icarus97). Such bodies once belonged to the main belt of minor planets but were knocked out of this belt by the strong and perturbing influence of Jupiter's gravity.

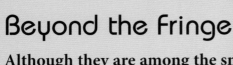

Beyond the Fringe

Although they are among the smallest bodies in the Solar System, comets are also among the oldest. Their origin is intimately linked to that of the system itself because they appear to have condensed directly from the primordial solar nebula material.

Although their appearance has traditionally been seen as an omen of doom, the prediction of the regular reappearance of comets was one of the first achievements of early astronomers. Today their return is celebrated by scientists as an exceptional opportunity to glean information about the early history of the Solar System.

Curriculum Context

For most curricula, students should be aware of the appearance, general composition, size, and motion of objects in the Solar System, including comets.

Comets have only a very small mass, which means that they have undergone little chemical differentiation since they formed. They are therefore thought to be relics of the primitive solar nebula material that accreted to form the outer planets.

Composition and orbit

Comets are composed of ice and dust and have been graphically described as "dirty snowballs." They may have originated in the outer reaches of the Solar System, near the present positions of Uranus and Neptune, but were gravitationally perturbed at an early stage, and probably thrown out into a vast cloud, of hundreds of billions of comets, that encircles the Solar System. This cloud, known as the Oort cloud, is found about one third of the distance to the nearest star. Some of these objects may become disturbed into shorter-period, but highly elliptical, orbits that bring them into the inner Solar System, though not necessarily in the same plane as the planets.

As a comet approaches the Sun, its icy nucleus partly vaporizes, generating a diffuse bright coma, or cloud of dust and gases, and a tail of gaseous particles, ionized

Comet NEAT appeared in northern skies in 2004. In this photo the comet's coma (the gas cloud around the nucleus) and the inner part of its tail are visible. A comet's coma may be 1 million miles (1.6 million km) in diameter, and the tail may extend 100 million miles (160 million km).

by the solar wind. The tail always points away from the Sun, and may be hundreds of millions of miles in length; it may appear very brilliant from Earth. A shorter second tail of dust particles "left behind" by the nucleus is sometimes also found.

Solar wind

The solar wind is a stream of charged particles that are ejected from the outer layers of the Sun and travel out through the Solar System.

Halley's comet

The passage of Halley's comet through the Solar System in 1986 was particularly informative because it allowed scientists to send five space probes (notably *Giotto*) directly into the heart of the comet. In doing so they learned that the nucleus was a tumbling, irregular-shaped mass 10 miles (16 km) long and 5 miles (8 km) wide, with a cratered surface. The surface was very dark. It seems that this darkening is induced when the comet passes close to the Sun, and the interior ices melt, causing a thick residue of "soot" to build up on the surface of the nucleus. Jets of gas were observed streaming out, sometimes erupting material at the rate of 11 tons (10 tonnes) per second. Spectroscopic studies confirmed that a cometary nucleus consists of carbonaceous materials and hydrated silicates, in a slushy matrix of water and other ices, such as methane, ammonia, and carbon dioxide.

Forming Cores

No one knows exactly how the planets formed. But, by making reasonable assumptions about early temperatures and pressures inside the Earth, and looking at the contribution made by radioactive elements, it becomes possible to make intelligent guesses about the process.

From these computations of early temperatures and pressures, geologists have concluded that the accretional and radioactive energy produced in the early stages was unable to escape fast enough to prevent the heating up of our planet. Consequently, around 3.5 billion years ago, the interior temperature was sufficiently high to cause the metallic iron at the core to melt. This had far-reaching effects. A similar process occurred on the other inner planets, though the timing may have been different.

Concentration of metals

Because the Earth and other inner planets almost certainly began accreting material after metallic and silicate grains had condensed out of the solar nebula, it is likely that metallic particles containing iron and nickel were accreted first, because of their greater density. Metallic elements are also more ductile (able to change their shape) than silicates (rocky materials). Thus, the iron-rich particles gravitated to form the cores, while the silicates were concentrated nearer to the surface and eventually accumulated to form the mantle.

As the proto-planets continued to grow, their gravity increased. Calculations show that the sinking of metallic iron within the Earth would have begun around the point at which one-eighth of the planet's mass had accrued: it is clear that core formation started well before the entire Earth had accreted.

Differentiation

Once the separation of iron and silicates had begun—a process called differentiation—the planets heated up even more quickly as gravitational energy was released. If accretion was very rapid, radiation of thermal energy into space would have slowed and internal heating accelerated. Earth's internal temperature must have risen at least 3600°F (2000°C) by the time the core had segregated.

We know that there are now sizable amounts of both iron oxide (FeO) and iron sulfide (FeS) within Earth's

Mars

Crust 31 miles (50 km)
Mantle 1147 miles (1846 km)
Core 920 miles (1480 km)

Crust 43 miles (70 km)
Mantle 839 miles (1350 km)
Core 186 miles (300 km)

Earth

Moon

Crust 25 miles (40 km)
Mantle 1814 miles (2920 km)
Core 2125 miles (3420 km)

Venus

Mercury

Mantle 373 miles (600 km)
st *ca.* 100 miles
) km)
Core 1118 miles (1800 km)

Crust 37 miles (60 km)
Mantle 1895 miles (3050 km)
Core 1826 miles (2940 km)

Mercury's core accounts for 40 percent of its volume. Measurements made in 2007 showed that it is liquid. Earth's core is only 15 percent of the total volume. Venus's core may be about 12 percent, similar to that of Earth. Studies in 2003 suggested that Mars has a "squishy" core, which moves with the "tides" caused by the Sun's gravity.

core. If these were present at an early stage, they would have depressed the melting point of the metal phase as opposed to the silicate materials. As a result, the iron and nickel could sink toward the core as molten droplets, while the silicate materials (which eventually formed the mantle) remained solid.

The Moon and the Earth—which are the only planetary bodies accessible to thorough exploration so far—are the only two bodies for which there is comprehensive geochemical data. The Moon is a satellite, but it is large enough to be compared with the terrestrial planets. It has a small iron-silicate core, which appears to have formed 4 billion years ago; its radius cannot be larger than 250 miles (402 km) (the Earth's core has a radius of 2165 miles, 3485 km). Core formation could have raised its temperature by a mere 18°F (10°C).

Other cores

Among the other inner planets, Mars is of lower density than Earth and its core is either less dense or smaller than Earth's. There is some doubt, but most scientists believe that Mars' core accounts for between 7 and 21 percent of the planet's total volume. Venus, on the other hand, being similar to the Earth in terms of mass, probably has a very similar internal structure; its core is partly molten and slightly smaller than Earth's. This contrasts with Mercury, which is approximately 15 percent too dense to have been derived from the same parent material as the other inner planets. Its core is disproportionately large, having a radius of approximately 1118 miles (1800 km). Some scientists have conjectured that its original mantle was stripped away during Mercury's early history.

How Atmospheres Evolved

The earliest atmospheres resulted from the accumulation of gases that escaped from the interiors of rocky planets. All the planets except Mercury have—or once had—atmospheres, although they vary greatly from planet to planet, due to the different conditions found on each.

Volcanic gases

Silicate minerals in the Earth's crust, such as micas and amphiboles, contain hydrogen and oxygen within their crystalline structure, usually in the form of hydroxyl groups. These hydrated silicates occur widely in crustal rocks and have also been found in blocks believed to have originated in the upper mantle. As the planet heated up, silicate materials of the mantle partially melted to form magmas. These contained volatiles (low-boiling-point substances), including nitrogen, carbon dioxide, water, and others. Together they rose toward the surface; as the gases expanded, they provided pressure for a volcanic eruption, which could often be explosive and caused the outpouring of lavas and eruption clouds containing hot vapor, especially water. Enough water would have been released in this way to fill the Earth's ocean basins, assuming that volcanic eruptions on the early Earth were as common as they are today.

In addition to the volatiles from the interior, some light gases may have arrived from infalling comets. These icy bodies, which formed in the far reaches of the Solar System, are rich in hydrogen, nitrogen, and carbon compounds. No doubt many of them collided with the Earth during the early years of its history.

Earth's early atmosphere

Earth's early atmosphere was very different from today's. Research on volcanic gases suggests that water

Mica
A colorless to black mineral that splits into thin sheets. It is found in some granite and schist rocks.

Amphiboles
A group of generally dark-colored rock-forming minerals, characterized by crystals that form a chainlike structure.

vapor, carbon dioxide, carbon monoxide, nitrogen, hydrogen chloride, and hydrogen were most abundant. Hydrogen, which is very light, quickly escaped into space. Some of the water vapor in the upper atmosphere was broken down by sunlight into hydrogen and oxygen, the latter escaping and

Evolution of Earth's Atmosphere

The Earth's primeval atmosphere was very different from today's. Hydrogen was present in the atmosphere from the planet's formation until about 3.5 billion years ago, but was gradually lost into space. Carbon dioxide made up about 80 percent of the total atmosphere at first, but as it became fixed in limestone rocks, it gradually diminished. Nitrogen became more abundant as it escaped from the Earth's interior.

Between 3 and 1.5 billion years ago, carbon dioxide concentrations fell; nitrogen reached its maximum level. The

earliest bacteria appeared, followed by blue-green algae (cyanobacteria); these could carry out anaerobic photosynthesis.

By about 2 billion years ago, free oxygen was beginning to accumulate in the air as a result of photosynthesis. By 300 million years ago, about 20 percent of the Earth's atmosphere was oxygen.

combining with gases like methane (CH_4) and carbon monoxide (CO) to form water (H_2O) and carbon dioxide (CO_2). Free oxygen, so vital to life on Earth, was not found until the beginning of photosynthesis, by which carbon dioxide is taken in and free oxygen released as an end product.

The inner planets

Geological and other evidence suggests that in the distant past the inner planets were much less different in their volatiles composition than today, and that the present diversity is a result of differences in planetary mass and temperature. Mercury, which has weak gravity and a high surface temperature, could never hold onto its volatiles. Venus may once have had a large amount of water, but the dense carbon dioxide atmosphere that built up caused surface temperatures to rise and the water to evaporate; the hydrogen and oxygen ions then dissociated under the strong sunlight, and the hydrogen escaped into space. On Mars, running and standing water once existed in sufficient amounts to have left many surface features; the planet exhibits large ice caps formed of water and carbon dioxide, and the atmosphere today is mainly carbon dioxide.

The gas giants

The gas giants, on the other hand, are themselves made up of light elements, their atmospheres forming a kind of chemical soup which precipitates clouds of varying colors. The dominant components are hydrogen and helium, with much smaller amounts of methane and ammonia. These are the gases that the warmer, less massive inner planets could not retain, and which were swept outward by the solar wind until they were captured by the strong gravitational fields of the giant planets.

Curriculum Context

For many curricula, students should know that evidence from geological studies of Earth and other planets suggests that Earth's early atmosphere was very different from today.

Glossary

Accretion The capture of gas, dust, and other material by a planet, star, or other massive body. The material is attracted to the surface by gravitational forces.

Accretional energy The energy produced by the impact of pieces of rock as they hit the surface of a forming planet.

Amphiboles A group of generally dark-colored rock-forming minerals, characterized by crystals that form a chainlike structure.

Antimatter Fundamental particles that have opposite properties to particles of ordinary matter, such as protons, neutrons, and electrons. If matter and antimatter particles meet, they destroy each other in a burst of energy.

Antiparticle All fundamental particles have a matching antiparticle that has opposite characteristics. For example, the antiparticle to the electron is the positively charged positron. If a particle collides with its antiparticle, the two are annihilated.

Astrometric binary A bright star with a much dimmer companion, whose presence is detected through a "wobble" in the orbit of the brighter star.

Black holes Objects in space that are so dense that nothing can escape from them—not even light itself. A black hole has such a powerful gravitational field that any stars, gas clouds, dust, or other matter that stray too close are swallowed up.

Cepheid variables Cepheid variables are stars with masses between 5 and 20 times that of the Sun. They oscillate between two states. In one of the states the star is compact; in the other it expands and is much larger.

Compressional fault scarp A scarp (cliff or steep slope) produced when compressional forces cause rocks to fault or fracture, and one side of the fracture becomes raised above the other.

Electron degeneracy pressure The outward pressure from electrons that cannot occupy the same energy levels, which resists the tendency of matter to collapse further during a supernova.

Emission nebula A glowing cloud of hot interstellar gas. The gas is ionized (charged), and emits light of various colors (most often red, due to the presence of hydrogen).

Emission spectrum The different wavelengths of light produced by a source of light. Emission spectra can be used as an analytical tool. Lines within the spectrum at particular wavelengths indicate the presence of particular gases.

Halo The halo of a galaxy is a large spherical region that extends beyond the visible area of the galaxy. It contains some stars, and beyond these in the corona, hot gases.

Hubble flow The general movement of galaxies and clusters of galaxies away from observers on Earth, resulting from the expansion of the Universe.

Isotopes Atoms of the same element (i.e. with the same number of protons in the nucleus), but different numbers of neutrons.

Light-year The distance traveled by light, moving at 186,000 miles/sec (300,000 km/sec), in 1 year. One light-year is a distance of about 59 trillion miles (95 trillion kilometers) or 63,240 AU.

Lithosphere The rocky outermost layer of a planet, consisting of the crust and the upper mantle.

Meteorite A meteoroid (an asteroid on an Earth-crossing trajectory) that reaches the Earth's surface.

Mica A colorless to black mineral that splits into thin sheets. It is found in some granite and schist rocks.

Neutrinos Subatomic particles with an extremely low mass and no electric charge, which move at close to the speed of light. Neutrinos can pass through matter without interacting with it, which makes them very difficult to detect.

Neutron star A very dense star remnant that is all that is left of a large star after a supernova.

Nuclear fusion A nuclear reaction (i.e. one between atomic nuclei) in which hydrogen nuclei fuse (join together) to form helium nuclei. There is some loss of mass, which is converted into a large release of energy.

Photon A very small "packet" of light energy. At small scales, light can behave either like a particle or like a wave. A photon is a light "particle."

Planetesimals Small solid celestial bodies that are thought to have been the "seeds" of the planets.

Prominences Huge streamers of hot gas that break free from the Sun's surface and flare out into the corona. They are also known as solar flares.

Protostar A hot ball of gas that has not yet grown large enough or hot enough for fusion to begin in its core.

Quasar Quasi-stellar radio source. A very distant galaxy, not detectable in visible light, that is a strong source of radio waves.

Radioactive isotopes Atoms with unstable nuclei that decay (break down) by release of either particles or energy from the nucleus. The release of nuclear material is termed radioactivity.

Red shift A Doppler shift in the wavelength of light toward longer wavelengths produced when luminous objects (such as distant galaxies) are moving rapidly away from the observer.

Retrograde orbit An orbit that goes "backward," i.e. in the opposite direction to that of other planets, moons, or satellites.

Solar wind The solar wind is a stream of charged particles that are ejected from the outer layers of the Sun and travel out through the Solar System.

Spacetime continuum A mathematical model that combines space and time. Einstein developed this in his general theory of relativity.

Spectral lines (absorption lines) Dark lines in the spectrum (range) of light given out by a star. The lines are produced when certain wavelengths are absorbed by elements in the outer layers of the star.

Spectroscopic binary A binary star system detected by fluctuations of the spectral lines in the emission spectrum of a star.

Stellar wind A flow of neutral or charged gases from the upper atmosphere of a star. The gases may travel at speeds of hundreds of miles per second.

Strong nuclear force The force that holds the particles in the atomic nucleus together. Over very short distances, the strong force overcomes the electromagnetic repulsion between protons.

Volatiles Elements and molecules with low boiling points, which normally exist in gaseous form.

Weak nuclear force A weak force in the nucleus that is associated with radioactive decay.

Further Research

BOOKS

Couper, Heather, and Nigel Henbest. *The History of Astronomy*. Richmond Hill, Ontario: Firefly Books, 2007.

Dickinson, Terence. *Exploring the Night Sky: The Equinox Astronomy Guide for Beginners*. Richmond Hill, Ontario: Firefly Books, 1987.

Dinwiddie, Robert, Philip Eales, David Hughes, Ian Nicholson, Ian Ridpath, Giles Sparrow, Pam Spence, Carole Stott, Kevin Tildsley, and Martin Rees. *Universe*. New York: DK Adult, 2005.

Gribbin, John. *The Universe: A Biography*. New York: Penguin, 2008.

Kau, Michio. *Einstein's Cosmos: How Albert Einstein's Vision Transformed Our Understanding of Space and Time*. New York: W.W. Norton & Co., 2005.

Lintott, Chris, Brian May, and Patrick Moore. *Bang! The Complete History of the Universe*. Baltimore: Johns Hopkins University Press, 2008.

Nicolson, Iain. *Dark Side of the Universe: Dark Matter, Dark Energy, and the Fate of the Universe*. Baltimore: Johns Hopkins University Press, 2007.

Potter, Christopher. *You Are Here: A Portable History of the Universe*. New York: Harper, 2009.

Solway, Andrew. *Quantum Leaps and Big Bangs*. Chicago: Heinemann Library, 2007.

Sparrow, Giles. *The Planets: A Journey Through the Solar System*. London: Quercus, 2009.

PLANISPHERE

A planisphere is a map of the night sky that you can adjust to show how the sky will look at a particular time on a particular night of the year.

Chandler, David S. *The Night Sky 30°–40°* a two-sided planisphere. Springville, CA: David Chandler Co., 1997.

DVDS

Cohen, Douglas (director). *The Universe—The Complete Season One.* History Channel, 2007.

Cohen, Douglas (director). *The Universe—The Complete Season Two.* History Channel, 2008.

NOVA: Is There Life on Mars? WGBH Studio, Boston, 2009.

INTERNET RESOURCES

NASA Home. The NASA website is a huge resource that covers astronomy, Earth sciences, and space exploration. If you just want to browse, the home page is a good place to start.
www.nasa.gov/

NASA Johnson Space Center. A good starting point for anything related to manned space missions.
www.nasa.gov/centers/johnson/home/

Spitzer Space Telescope. The infrared Spitzer Space Telescope produces many spectacular images from the Milky Way and beyond.
www.spitzer.caltech.edu/spitzer/index.shtml

Astronomy Picture of the Day. Each day a different image or photograph of the Universe is featured, along with a brief explanation written by a professional astronomer.
http://apod.nasa.gov/apod/

Nine Planets. An overview of the history, mythology, and current scientific knowledge of the planets, moons, and other objects in our Solar System.
www.nineplanets.org/

The Nine 8 Planets. A version of the Nine Planets website revamped for a younger audience.
http://kids.nineplanets.org/

SPACE.com Space News. A good place to keep up to date with the latest developments in astronomy and space science.
www.space.com/news/

Index

Page numbers in **bold** refer to full articles; page numbers in *italic* refer to illustrations and captions.

A

Abell 901/902 (supercluster) *31*
absorption lines *see* spectral lines
accretion *77*
accretion disk 34, 35, *35*, 66, 68
accretion of planets **73–75**, 92, 97, 101
active galaxy 22, **32–35**
amino acids 52
ammonia 76, 90, 91, 99, 105
amphibole 103
Andromeda galaxy 8, 20, 29
Antarctica 87, 88
antimatter 16, 17
antineutrino 12, 16
antiparticle *10–11*, 11, 15, 16
aphelion 78
Apollo 17 mission *83*
asteroid 74, 76, **95–97**
astrometric binary 49
astronomers 6, 19, 27, 30, 33, 45, 52, 66, 70, 71, 87, 98
astronomical unit (AU) 7, 79
atmosphere 86, 94, **103–105**, *104*
atom 9, 10, 19, 56

B

Barnard object 53
barred spiral galaxy 24, *24*, 29
baryons 11, 17, 18, 64, 65, 68
basin 78, 82, 83
Becklin–Neugeberger object 54
Betelgeuse 44
Big Bang 6, 7–8, **9–14**, *10–11*, *14*, 15, 16, 17, 19, 20, 71, *72*
Big Bang timeline *14*
Big Crunch 70
Big Dipper 57
binary star system **49–51**, *50*, 66, 68, *68*
black dwarf 59
black hole 22, 25, 29, 34, **67–68**, 69
blazar 33, 34, 35
blue giant (star) 39, 44
blue supergiant (star) 68
Bok globules 53, *56*
brightness 38
brown dwarf 25, 38, 69
bubble chamber *61*
Bullet cluster 26

C

Callisto 93, *94*
Caloris Basin 84
carbon 103
carbon dioxide 99, 104, 105
carbon fusion 62
carbon monoxide 104, 105
carbon nucleus (star) 58, 60, 62
carbonaceous asteroid 96
carbon–nitrogen–oxygen reaction 60
Cassini 91, 92, 93
cD (cluster-dominating) galaxy 30
celestial equator 81
Cepheid variable star 58–59
Ceres 95
Chandrasekhar limit 65
Charon 79
chondrites 97
chondrules 97
chromosphere 41–43, *42*
classification of galaxies **23–24**
closed Universe 70, *70*
collapsar 67
coma 98, *99*
comet 74, 77, 79, 88, **98–99**, *99*, 103
constellations 38, 79
core (planetary) 82, 84, 90, 92, 100, 101, *101*, 102
core collapse 63
core (Sun) *42*
corona (Sun) *42*, 43
coronae (Venus) 85
cosmic (microwave) background radiation 12, *18*, 19, 71
cosmological constant 72
cosmos 19, 21, 72
Crab nebula 66
crater 78, 82, 84, 85, 86
critical density 70
crust (planetary) 84, 86, *101*
Cygnus X-1 68

D

Dark Ages *14*, 21, 22
dark energy 72
dark matter 26, *26*, 69, 72
Dawn space probe 96
decoupling (matter and energy) 12, 19, 20
degenerate matter 64, 66
density 82, 84, 86
deuterium 18
differentiation 101
"dirty snowballs" 98
distance measurement 62, 71

D (continued)

Doppler effect 51
dwarf planet 7, 92
dwarf star 46

E

Earth 7, *7*, 25, *28*, 34, 38, 41, 43, 49, 62, 64, 68, 71, 73, 77, *77*, 78, 79, 80, *80–81*, 81, **82–83**, 84, 85, 86, 87, 88, 89, 90, 91, 93, 94, 95, 96, 97, 98, 100, 101, *101*, 102, 103, 104, 105
Earth's atmosphere 103–104, *104*
eccentricity *80–81*
eclipse (solar) 43
Einstein, Albert 72
electromagnetic force 9, 13, 15, 69
electron 9, *10–11*, 12, 15, 17, 18, 19, 41, 43, 56, 64, 69
electroweak force 11
Elephant's trunk nebula *54*
elliptical galaxy 21, 22, 23–24, *24*, 30, 37
emission nebula 57
energy 7, 11, 12, 13, 15, 18, *18*, 19, 20, 22, 34–35, 38, *45*, 46, 47, 48, 53, 54, 55, 57, 58, 59, 60, 61, *61*, 62, 63, 65, 68, 71, 72, 74, 77, 78, 100, 101
equinox 81
Eris 92
Eros 95
escape velocity 67
Europa 92, 93, *94*
event horizon 67
expansion of Universe 11, 19, 31, 43, 69, 70, 71, 72, *72*, 73
exponents 7

F

flat Universe 70, *70*
formation of Moon 83
formation of Solar System 73–75, *74–75*
fossilized bacteria 89
fragmentation (asteroid) 95–96
fusion, nuclear 19, 38, 48, 55, 57, 58, 60, 67

G

galactic center 28–29
galactic collision *21*, **36–37**, *37*
galaxy 6, 8, 12, 19, **20–40**, 52, 62, *63*
galaxy cluster 6, *8*, **30–31**, *31*, 69

galaxy formation **30–32**
Galileo 92, 93
Galileo Galilei 27
Ganymede 93, 94
gas cloud 35, 36, 52
gas giants 74, 75, 105
grand unified theory (GUT) force 11, 13
granulation 41
gravitational lensing *26*
gravity 9, 13, 15, 19, 20, 23, 49, 52, 53, 55, 60, 64, 67, 68, 70, 72, 82, 95, 97, 105
gravity well 34
Great Dark Spot 91
Great Red Spot 90
Great Wall (supercluster) 31
greenhouse effect 85

H

half-life 77
Halley's comet 99
halo stars 40
halo, galactic 25, 26, 40
helium 12, 38, 39, 43, 48, 58, 60, 61, 76, 90, 105
helium fusion 58
Herbig–Haro object 55
Hertzsprung–Russell diagram 47, *47*, 48, 55
Hubble Space Telescope (HST) 22, 91
Hubble, Edwin 6, 23
Huygens 92, 93
hydrogen 12, 18, 38, 48, 52, 53, 56, 57, 58, 70, 76, 90, 91, 103, 104, 105
hydrogen chloride 104

I

ice cap 86
inflation (of Universe) 11, **13–14**
infrared (IR) radiation 22, 28, 32, 44, 54
inner planets 74, **84–85**, 103, 105
interstellar gas/dust 23, 25,39
inverse square law 62
Io 92, 93, 94
ionization 19
ionization 43
ions 43, 105
iron 102
iron core (star) 62
iron oxide 101
iron sulfide 101
irregular galaxy 24
Ishtar Terra 85
isotope 77

J

James Webb Space Telescope 22
jets (radiation) 34
Jovian planets **90–92**
Jupiter 76, *77*, **78–81**, *80–81* 90, *90–91*, 91, 92, 93, 95, 97

K

Kepler, Johannes *63, 78*
Kepler supernova remnant *63*

L

lava 83, 93
laws of planetary motion 78
layers of the Sun 42
lenticular galaxy 24, *24*
leptons 9, 13, 15
lighthouse model *65*, 66
light, speed of 16. 67, 69
light-year 7
Local Group 8, 29, 30, 31
luminosity 32, 38, 48, 55, 69

M

M-class asteroid 96
Maffei I (galaxy) 29
Magellan 85, *85*
magma 103
magnetic field 43, 56, 66
main sequence stars 46–47, *47*, **55–57**, 58, 60
mantle (planet) 83, 84, 100, *101*, 103
maria ("seas") 82, 83
Mariner 10 84
Mars *77*, **78–81**, *80–81*, 84, 95, 102, 105
    life on **87–89**
    water on 88, 89

Mars Global Surveyor 89
Mars missions 89
Mars Odyssey 88
mass 39, 46, 49, 56, 62, 64, 65, 68, 69, 74, 91
matter 9, 11, 12, 13, 15, 16, 17, *18*, 19, 20, 21, 24,25, 26, 31, 34, 38, 53, 54, 55, 57, 58, 59, 60, 61, *61*, 63, 65, 68, 71, 72, 74, 77, 78, 100, 101
Maxwell Montes 85
Mercury 7, *77*, **78–81**, *80–81*, 84, 93, 102, 103
metals 39, 100, 102
meteor 78
meteorite 76, 77, 88, 97

meteoroid 74, 95, 96
methane 76, 91, 99, 105
mica 103
Milky Way 6, 8, 20, **27–29**, *28*, 30, 32, 38, 39, 40, 63, 73
molecular cloud 53, 57
Moon **82–83**, 102
Moon rock *83*
moons 73, 92, **93–94**
multiple star system 51

N

NASA 87
NEAR 95
NEAT comet *99*
Neptune 76, *77*, **78–81**, *80–81*, 90, *90–91*, 91, 92, 93, 94, 98
neutrino 9, *10–11*, 12, 15, 16, *16* , 63, 69
neutron 9, *10–11*, 12, 15, 16, 17, 18, 64, 69
neutron star 25, 38, 63, **64–66**, 67, 68
nitrogen 103, 104
North Pole 81
nucleosynthesis 17, **60–61**
nucleus, atomic 9, 13, 18, 41, 58, 60, 61, 77
nucleus, comet 98, 99
nucleus, galaxy 23, 24, 26, 29, 32, 35, 39, 40

O

O and B type stars 56, *56*, 57
obliquity 80
ocean 93, 103
omega (W) 70
Oort cloud 98
open Universe 70, *70*
Oppenheimer–Volkhoff limit 65, 67
orbit 26, 27, 39, 49, *50*, 51, 52, 57, 64, 70, 75, 78, 79, 80, *80–81*, 84, 86, 87, 91, 92, 95, 98
Orion (arm) 27, 28
oxygen 104, 105

P

parsec 7
particle accelerator *61*
Pauli exclusion principle 64
perihelion 78
Perseus (arm) 27, 28
phases of Moon 82
Phoenix 89

photon 10, 19, 45, 69
photosphere 41, 43, *42*, 45, 46
photosynthesis 104, 105
Piazzi, Guiseppe 95
Planck curves 45
Planck time 10
planet 12, 73, 75, **78–81**, *80–81*, 87, 91, 98, 105
planetary nebula 59, *59*
planetary rotation 80, 90
planetary structure **100–102**
planetesimal 73, 74–75, *74–75*, 82, 83
Pleiades 57
Pluto 7, 8, 73, *77*, 78, *80–81*, 92
polar ice 87
Population I stars 39
Population II stars 38, 39, 40
positron 17
precession 80
prominences *42*, 43
proton 9, *10–11*, 12, 15, 16, 17, 18, 43, 56, 60, 61, 64, 69
proton–proton chain 61
protostars 53–54, 55, 66, 73
proto-Sun 76, 77, 84
Proxima Centauri 8
pulsar **65–66**, *65*

Q

quarks 9, *10–11*, 11, 13, 15, 16
quasar (quasi-stellar radio source) 32, 34
quasi-stellar object (QSO) 32

R

radio galaxy 33,34
radio lobes 34, 35
radioactive isotope 77, 101
red dwarf 46, 57
red giant (star) 44, 48, 50, 58, 71
red shift 6, 30, 32, 71, 72
regolith 74
retrograde motion 85
Riga 44
ring system 90, 91
Rosette nebula *56*

S

Sagittarius (arm) 27, 28
Sagittarius A* 28–29
satellite 103
Saturn 76, *77*, **78–81**, *80–81* 90, *90–91*, 91, 92, 93
Schwarzschild radius 67
seasons 81
Seyfert, Carl 32

Seyfert galaxy 32, 34
shepherd moon 91
shooting star 96
silicates 76, 84, 99, 100, 102, 103
singularity 67
Sirius A, Sirius B 49
smog 94
SNC meteorite 97
solar nebula 73, 75, 76, 77, 97, 98, 100
solar spectrum 43
Solar System 6, 7, 8, 22, 25, 41, 43, 54, 73, 75, 76, 77, **78–81**, 93, 95, 97, 99, 103
solar wind 43, 99, 105
solstice 81
space probe 85, 86, 87, 91, 93
spacetime 6, 69, 70
spectral lines 6, 35, 45, 51
spectroscopic binary 51
spectroscopy 45, 99
spectrum (star) **44–45**
speed of light 16, 67, 69
spinning up 66
spiral arms 22, 24, 25, 27, 29, 39, 40, 53
spiral galaxy 21, 22, 23–24, *24*, 25, 27, 30, 33, 36, 38
Spitzer Space Telescope *54*
star 6, 7, 8, 12, 18, 19, 20, 21, 22, 23, 24, 25, 26, 27, 29, 32, 34, 36, 37, *37*, **38–66**, *39*, *47*, *50*, *56*, *59*, *65*, 67, 68, *68*, 71, 77, 78, 79, 98
star classification 44
star clusters 57
star color **44–45**, *45*, *47*
star evolution 57, *59*
star formation 36, 37, **52–54**
star temperature 45, 46, 47
starburst 36
stellar wind *50*, 56
strong nuclear force 9, 11, 12, 13, 16
S-type asteroid 96
Sudbury Neutrino Detector *16*
sugars 52
Sun 7, *7*, 8, 12, 20, 27, 28, *28*, 39, 40, **41–43**, *42*, 44, 46, 47, *47*, 48, 53, 57, 58, 59, 60, 61, 64, 65, 67, 73, 77, *77*, 78, 79, 80, *80–81*, 82, 84, 86, 90, 91, 92, 95, 98, 99, 101
sunspots 41
supercluster 21, 30–31
superforce10, *10–11*,
supernova 22, 39, **62–63**, 64, 65, 66, 71, 72, 77

T

tail (comet) 98, 99, *99*
telescope 20, 22, 44, 48, 87, 91, 96
tesserae 86
tides 82
Titan 92, 93, 94
torus 34, 35
Trans-Neptunian objects *77*, 78, 92
triple alpha process 61
tritium 18
Triton 92
"tuning fork" diagram 23, *24*

U

ultraviolet (UV) radiation 43, 44
Uranus 76, *77*, **78–81**, *80–81* 90, *90–91*, 91, 92, 93, 94, 98

V

Valles Marinaris 86
Venera 86
Venus *77*, **78–81**, *80–81*, 84, *85*, 102, 105
Viking 87
Virgo supercluster 8, 31
voids 31
volatiles 76, 77, 86, 92, 97, 103, 105
volcanic eruption 103
volcanoes 85, 86, 88, 92, 93
Voyager 91, 92

W

water 76, 86, 91
water vapor 104, 105
wavelength 22, 28, 32, 34, 35, 42, 44, 45, 51, 54, 56, 59, 65, 71
weak nuclear force 9, 13, 15
weighing stars 51
white dwarf 38, 46, 47, 48, 49, 59, *59*, 64, 66, 67, 68, 71
WIMPs (weakly interacting massive particles) 69
WMAP (Wilkinson Microwave Anisotropy Probe) 18

X

X rays 34, 43, 68
X-ray telescope 22